MAO'S MOLE

Marc Vincenz

NeoPoiesisPress.com

NeoPoiesis Press, LLC

2775 Harbor Ave SW
Suite D
Seattle, WA 98126-2138

Inquiries:
P.O. Box 38037
Houston, TX 77238-8037

NeoPoiesisPress.com

Marc Vincenz – Mao's Mole
ISBN 978-0-9892018-1-0 (pbk)
     978-0-9892018-4-1 (hardcover)
     1. Poetry. I. Vincenz, Marc. II. Mao's Mole.

Library of Congress Control Number: 2013949975

First Edition

Cover, design and typography: Milo Duffin and Stephen Roxborough

Printed in the United States of America

für meine kleine feine unberechenbare Familie

Foreword

At the beginning of this book our poet is climbing the Kunlun Mountains, paradise of the Taoists, mythical source of the Yellow River. And, "naturally, as you might expect," an old man materializes from behind a tree. He leads our poet to the expected cave, shows him the expected book with the names and specifications of "anyone who has ever dared live." Our poet finds his entry, and what does it comprise? Nothing less than the 111 poems of *Mao's Mole*. Subsumed under the rubric Marc Vincenz is the most exhaustive yet intimate rendering of modern China in all of Indo-European poetry. He has literally made this infinite civilization his own. It's a just claim.

In the first poem, Cixi, the last Empress Dowager, is disdaining her "useful dolts" as they kowtow to the billiard table which Queen Victoria has given her. From there, *Mao's Mole* sweeps all the way forward to the millennium we upstart occidentals quaintly call our "third." Along the way, Mao himself, poetaster tutelary and eponymous bugaboo, makes his entrance. Still young, wan, thin and affable, he stands on top of the Exalted Mountain, and proclaims the east to be that certain notorious hue, only to wind up "vacuum-sealed, embalmed, death defying" in his crystal casket. A couple blocks away, "Starbucks yawns wide behind the knobbed doors of heaven."

Meanwhile, *naturally*, as you might expect, Deng Xiaoping pops up, hawking his Socialism with Chinese Characteristics. In Marc Vincenz's revision, the superannuated dwarf must deal with a contingent of Shaolin monks who show up at the Tiananmen Square massacre "shooting thunderbolts from their fingers." Deng's dictum about the glory of getting rich inspires schemes of karaoke bars in Shanghai's old alleys; but his touted modernization fails to confiscate shards of dragon eggshells from a rural child, urbanized but not cured of feudal superstition.

As always in any Marc Vincenz book there are the lovely women, fresh with "tiny pinprick breasts like ripe buds of corn," and, of course, the food. In this case, it's the street stall cuisine we expatriates have known so well: *spitting seeds and bits of rind, where fish heads and spines lay rotting amongst flies*. Accommodations are provided courtesy of hotels with names like Red Star, where you must battle the rats for rights to the apple, compliments of the manager.

Mao's Mole has much truck with factories and their managers, for our poet himself spent over ten years in that purgatory, in cahoots with bankers and party muckety-mucks, steeped in corruption of such labyrinthine intensity as can only be achieved in the world's oldest continuous bureaucracy. Naturally, as you might expect, the poetry achieves some of its highest pitches in these unpoetic circumstances:

...it's all leaching under the foundations
can't let the shareholders know or the factory would close
I just smiled back & cheered our good health—

The world was big & cancer was everywhere
in the meat, in the bread, the sky, the unflinching earth
only in Iceland will the volcanoes get you

& then there was factory kingpin Ying
with the blue phone glued to his ear—
he who rose from the communist earth

In his previous collection, *Gods of a Ransacked Century* (Unlikely Books), Marc Vincenz gave us a full cosmology, from the materia prima of tachyon waves to hydrogen bombs and rocket salads. He provides nothing less in *Mao's Mole*. The people of the Flowery Middle Kingdom have long considered their walled world coextensively coterminous with the cosmos, relegating any outliers to triviality and irrelevance. Marc Vincenz is one of the few barbarians who has entered and encompassed their universe.

Having lived and wandered there for some years, I can affirm that Marc Vincenz's is the clearest, most intelligent and emotionally intense evocation of that unfathomable place I've ever read in verse or prose. "Everything is on these pages, the poisoned as well as the pristine, all presented with hallucinatory concision by one of the the the strongest living poets in our language."

—Tom Bradley

Table of Contents

I. Changing the Pear

II. Paper Tigers

III. One Hundred Flowers Bloom

IV. Our Father Who Art in People's Square

V. The Buddha's Last Firecrackers

Down with imperialism
Down with imperialism
Eliminate the warlords
Eliminate the warlords
Revolution will triumph
Revolution with triumph
All sing together
All sing together

Nationalist Chinese Song, 1920

(Sung to the tune of "*Frère Jacques*")

World in disorder? Excellent situation.

—Mao Zedong

Quest

Kunlun Mountains, Qinghai, 1989

Foot in front of foot, you say.
Don't look up: observe the weed,

the flutter of the onionskin flies.
Pretend we climb for the divine

where wise men are locked tight,
hidden from light on the incline,

evolve universes in their mind.
Just above the treeline, water

boils in slow plops & we abandon rice,
sucking caramel & chocolate, chewing gum.

On the other side goats bound, sugar-mad,
bleat wild between tufts & crags

& an old man peeks from behind a tree.
Naturally—as you might expect—

he says, *follow me, follow me,*
& leads us to his cave where fire crackles.

& the old man, mumbling, produces a book,
leather frayed on its leaves; in gold

lie splayed the names of anyone
who has ever dared live, catalogued

soul by single soul, place and time of birth.
Scribbled in a corner, I find mine. It reads:

Changing the Pear

*If you want knowledge, you must take part
in the practice of changing reality.
If you want to know the taste of a pear,
you must change the pear by eating it yourself.*

—*Mao Zedong*

The Dowager Empress Admires Her New Billiard Table,

a Gift from Queen Victoria, Hall of the Graceful Bird,
Zhongnanhai, Beijing, 1899

I too have my
useful dolts

mostly men
punched up

on sorghum brandy
clicking clacking

kowtow
like billiards balls

bungling into
all the wrong holes

Old Cathay

Janice and George wheeze up mountains
and cross into a past

Doctor Foo says only he knows,
where pandas chew wild bamboo

and once-red-guards plough rice paddies
with water-snorting buffalo, horns tippling wide to side.

And a crouched prune of a man with a burning root in his mouth
invites all to see the future in joss sticks

smoking towards his ancestors,
beyond snow and mountain, and brings rains.

He clucks so like a rooster that all the chicken waddle in—
strokes them like loved mongrels returning back from the fields

and breaks their necks tenderly with a single motion
of his watchless wrist, plucks them in less time

than it takes to light another cigarette, and when ready,
bears his receded gums and one gold tooth for measure.

Taishan Mountain

On Revolution: You must not move with excessive haste,
nor use excessive ruthlessness against the people.
—*I-Ching, The Book of Changes*

On Taishan Mountain behind the fog
we wait for first glimpses of dawn.

It's here, hovering on China's precipice,
the Chairman proclaims the East is Red,

deems himself ruler of all he beholds.
I'm standing right beside him.

We've just fought a war; he's so thin,
and he has this steely glint

as if he's stumbled across some great illumination.
It's a moment of connection with the universe,

a revelation beyond normal human comprehension,
something to make history, like Einstein

unraveling the universal laws
of energy and mass and motion.

In this moment I know nothing will ever be the same again.
I know he has to tear the world apart at the seams,

fold it back upon itself to find his true place in it.
Everything for love, he says.

He breathes in, as if trying to capture the last
essence of olden sky, and as often, he considers

one of his heroes, Karl Marx, and what that bearded
wonder might have said on a day such as this,

in a definitive moment such as this.
And you won't believe it,

but he turns from the spectacle
of nature illuminating before us,

the hills, the valley, the forest below and faces me full-on,
grabs my head in his smoky hands and plants a huge,
            wet kiss on my lips,

then says: *We've all got to move on. You know, Richard,
you've got to get rid of that damn moustache.*

Lovers Arrested

If you had been there voicing your opinions
like the rest of us I might have fallen in love with you.

If you had taken the effort to plaster a slogan or
wave a flag from the rooftops I might have learned to.

If you had bellowed your freedom of speech and turned your thoughts
into something that mattered I might have seen you as a man.

She's packing her bag—socks, panties, and would you believe?
those patchwork flannel pajamas made by her mother,

the ones she wears Sundays to kick around the house—
with the police waiting outside.

If you'd held my hand as we faced the wall of tyranny,
or rubbed my back to spur me on.

Isn't it for the man to protect the woman?
She had something there.

And I wasn't even helping her pack.
And what did you tell them?

I pass her toothbrush, shampoo, a pair of nail clippers
which I know they'll confiscate.

You told them it was nothing to do with you. With *you*!
The law, after all, you said, is always the law.

That's just like saying you don't mind my affairs.
Could you really stand another man inside me?

I want to kiss her before she leaves.
I want to hug her from every side.

She zips it up like it's everything she has, and says:
Sometimes I think you're no man at all.

Democracy Wall

—for Wei Jingsheng and Huang Xiang

Look what's pasted here—

Poet on the wall says
we're all dictators, despots
shouldering to get in first.

Old men
with inflated superegos.

Besides, what the fuck does he know?
He's only a lad.
Enlightened poets carve their
words in stone—
these just whimper,
blow away like leaves
in a storm.

He might as well
scratch them
in the sky.

Commission for The Protection of Party Secrets

after the Five-year Review of the National Congress Assembly

*We shall now follow the principles of Communism with Chinese
characteristics.*
—Deng Xiao Ping

Let me tell you a secret,
he whispers in the long corridor—

perhaps he's hoping echoes will not muffle his intentions,
but amplify his way of saying things between things.

You'd think by now he'd have printed a cipher
he could hand out at official Party functions.

Secret is a word he bandies around like it's a promise or a clue.
Perhaps he's re-composing himself?
or is he just trying to heighten surface tension?

Now he finally stops in front, sixty-even echoes beyond the guard room.
A secret about a secret, here?

Keep walking, Comrade.
I prefer to observe from behind.

While Facing the Urinal

Where a Placard Reads, 'Come Closer. We Don't Want You Watering Your Shoes.' Public Toilet behind the Second District Police Station, Ningbo, 2004

A man in a public toilet
        once asked me
if there was anyone
        I needed to have done.

I asked what he meant,
        told him I couldn't read
between lines, especially
        when I was trying to have a piss.

& he said, anything you don't want:
        an arm, a leg, an eye, a head,
I can have it disappear like magic,
        made into fertilizer, mixed with pig dung.

Rice crops thrive on human meat.
        Just think of all the wars
that have helped it replenish, he said.
        I was still not clear, and as I

shook down, pulled up my zip,
        he had his hands in the Swedish
blow-drier mounted on the wall.
        And he said, It's all a matter of price.

Three hundred for an arm, five for a leg,
        a paltry thousand for a head.
Dwell on it well, he said.
        No need to make decisions now,

But call me when the need arises.
In business sometimes
you need to teach lessons,
and some are only learned

by losing something.
He'd left his name card
sitting on the edge of the sink,
And it got wet,

and the ink smeared,
so in the end all I got
was a number,
but I never caught a name.

Measuring the Gods

Four Winds Vacuum Cleaner Plant, Site of New Workshop, Pudong,
Shanghai, 2004

1. The Ch'i of yin and yang breathes out as wind, rises up as clouds,
*   descends as rain, and courses underground as vital energy.*
2. Earth is the receptacle of C'hi—where there is earth, there is Ch'i.
3. Ch'i is the mother of water—where there is C'hi, there is water.
4. The Classic says: Ch'i flows where the earth changes shape;
*   the flora and fauna are thereby nourished*
*   — Guo Pu (276-324 A.D.)*

The feng shui compass sits   in the old man's hands
as he bungles through rubble   in his soiled Mephistos
teetering like a toddler

for fifty-odd years, he says,   I've been divining
of gods.   measuring the intention

                                       At every twitch
of the needle   he shakes, mumbles, notates:

No, no, this is entirely wrong,   you need your back flush
up against the mountain,   facing the water flow
to entice the money in.

And this wall must come down,   it's blocking all the *C'hi.*

The architect is baffled   and whispers to the contractor
who plugs his calculator   with his own intention.
A sheen of concentration   beads on the old man's pate.

He reaches for a striped hanky,   pats his furrows, sits down
on a dusty bamboo stool   which appears from nowhere.

Can't you feel it?   The ceiling is all wrong.
It needs to come up   at least three centimeters.

Now the contractor's really clucking.

& here, above the door points the old man,
it needs to be covered in reflective surfaces,
force out evil spirits, else this will be the desk
of a poor man.

by the elbow as he rises. They support him

And then he curses:

Oh, in the name of the Immortals,
where is that damned green dragon?

Advanced Tree-Planting

*after-evening sessions at the Xingang
Communist Party offices*

Comrade Fa says:

Grassroots democratic politics
is like water:

You have to channel it
to stop the flooding:

The people have to know
they're getting something

for all their back-
breaking work.

She Thinks I Look Like Lenin

My secret girlfriend asked me in a Beijing KFC:
Do you think that Marx would have liked Coca-Cola?

I imagined his face in place of Colonel Saunders.
And laughed, thinking of P F C: Proletariat Fried Chicken.

Do you know why Mao loved Marx so much? she asked.
Why, it was the beard, of course. He couldn't grow one.

And she went on nibbling her wing.

Wushu

Tiananmen Square, Beijing, June 4, 1989

In waking a tiger, use a long stick
—Mao Zedong

Tracers shred the sun
in swallow-streaks of red,
tank track crushes bicycle bones
to street fossil.

A river of bobbing heads.

Along the shore
heaving housewives jab the air,
teachers cluck,
workers on rooftops flash the birdie,
buses taxis rickshaw boys
wave flags of freedom.

Soon the Shaolin monks will arrive
shooting thunderbolts
from their fingers
& we'll stand firm,
shoulder to shoulder,
fist to raw fist.

We've been wrestling sleep for seven nights and days:
nothing but bitter tea leaves and dreams.

We're waiting for the final push,
the rip-roar, hold silent,
eyeing them down like their mothers,
then, the unknown man breaks rank,
treads down
the dotted line
as if he might walk
through steel—

Superstition 1976 (The Year He Died)

—for Li Zhisui, Chairman Mao's Personal Physician

in those last days
he drooled

regressing
into the dark

caves of Yan'an
where once he

dreamed poems
to smite foes

he had crossed
the Great Wall

a hundred times
and in the end

all he wanted
was a light

Roosters

Yu Fa to Yu Liu, 7.45 am, Bus Line 142 Hongxiao to Pudong, Shanghai, 2004

You can almost smell the dirt in her hair
among the flowers and the pollinating bees.

See the way the fabric falls so clumsily?
and her tiny pinprick breasts

like ripe buds of corn—she's fresh.
Got off the train this very morning.

Now she's off to her first city job
at the Red Rooster Noodle House.

See the way she wears her hair coiled in a tight bun?
Bet it's sweet like sugared red-bean-curd rolls

the way my Auntie Lu makes them
back in Shaanxi for Spring Festival.

Ah, Yu, admire her now, for soon
she will be serving up lunch

and the pink in her cheek
and the dimple in her chin

will all be watered down
into sweet melon soup, slurped

for a Buddha's lunch
in between belches and

cigarettes and
spicy beef noodles.

The Price of Humidity

Inner Ring Freeway, Shanghai, 2006

We've hit stone and the front right is flapping: a real live plucked
chicken. Yet, apparently unfazed, he drives on; strangely, he leans
to the left as if his scrawny body weight might balance the load.

The five of them, piled in behind, jumbles of sweaters,
and musty tweed, ties like stethoscopes, banded eels, liquorice twizzlers,
entrails, and I daren't say: one like a hangman's noose.

We're halted again, not from the flap of rubber, but there's a fight,
right in the middle of the road. Cars, trucks, motorbikes,
piles of produce perched and ready to spill;
still, they weave their way round, sputters,

toss a glance, flick an occasional butt, gravel, carbon-monoxide gust,
grumble, hoot, but the scrap ensues; fisticuffs.
One has a swinging Shaolin kick. *Ooo—crack straight to the jaw.*
Backseat basket crowd of five applauds.

A gold tooth clinks along the fender rail. Anyway, there's nowhere
to go. The fat one has the thin one pinned, flat foot of sole grinding,
oozing rust. Evening scrapes in, headlights pop on and eyes glint.

Behind me they're calling bets: five to one on Skinny, three to one
on Humpty, fresh notes are crackling, and there's nowhere to go;
full school bus straight ahead, passes, wheedling the barrier. Taxi left.

Skinny spins to hands, flips back, kick straight to the nose. Humpty
stumbles, two hands cupped like avian-flu mask, cracks, swings forth
in chops. Skinny steps on his shoe. Humpty reels, hops on one toe.

Again, the crowd applauds. Someone's raised the odds on Skinny,
paper changes hands. Guy with a tie like a noose, screams
from the window: *Onward Shaolin Master!*
Strike him down now! Squash him like a frog!

But the thin man, bends over, coughs three days of cigarettes,
hacks, then stands, steps calmly into his taxi and rumbles off.
Great boo and sigh behind.

Javier Blanco Reinvents Himself

*and Plants a Juicy Kiss on the Banks
of the Yellow River*

Suzhou, Jiangsu Province, 2005

Beneath the sharp pagoda—one thousand years of rising shadow,
cooling shade in August swelter, whale prick on asphalt—

looms over the surging swill of moss-green canals under cherry
blossoms yearning for spring, and those bloated bags, once vacuumed
      are now expired.

Pungency stirs humid like occidental perfume. You and Madame Hao
eye in eye, flutters and rosy cheeks, her hand dangled to graze
      the surface of water—

but she hesitates, slips, tilts, and splashes into the gunk of restaurants
and effluents known only in chemical symbols to Suzhou engineers.

Lucky, lucky for you the *Green Mile Roasted Duck*
is open for business, glitters in gold and red bangles, arched

in firecrackers, and that duck and goose fat dribbling
in the window likens the sheen of sweat now blistering beneath

your curly hairline. Madame Hao big-fish-dripping, reappears
vainglorious, resplendent like the dowager empress, tassels on sleeves
      and bells

on toes. She's smiling for the first time. *España tiene mucho hombre.
China é mucho mas lento.* You've got those hedgehog prickles
      through your feet

just like that first night in Madrid.

Tea and biscuits, and the trill
of zither and harp, followed by lashings of plum sauce, onion

and Peking duck; rattling A/C: cool gusts of ammonia, bleach and sorghum.
Soon the lunch crowd clatters and clinks, drowns out the silence

and the *clunk clunk clunk* of dim sum trolleys. You and the empress
are given a wide berth and ogle eyes, camera clicks, winks and mumbles

all the way back to Shanghai. You hold her clothes out the train
window until they dry, and when you arrive, you saunter down near

the really yellow river, hand takes clammy hand; you lean in, top heavy,
against the railing and kiss, straight between the eyes.
        Adios y mucho suerte.

You taxi home, alone, in the roar of gnashing jackhammers and
squeaky cranes, the grit of Shanghai hitting your teeth, and now, finally,
        night descends

and the scratch and crawl of bicycles is *ting-tinging.*

An email in your inbox:

Mucho hombre neccessito mucha mujer. Joint venture tomorrow.

Same time, same place. Be there. Waiting for your Spanish Kiss on my

Chinese lips again and again.

Beneath the sharp pagoda.

Hunchback Rat of the Red Star Hotel

Red Star Hotel, Kunlun, 1994

Rattled into the hotel room at three past one
Clunking: veteran sailor on one good leg.

Oh for the wave and break, the ten-past-one spins,
Fifteen-past draw of squall and flit,
Flit of tired moonlit eyes. And sometime,
When at last sun is inhaling, oxygenated in pink,

All, all is still, is still, is still, no land,
No land in sight, just wind, wind and sighs.

Yet peace, as any good sailor will grumble,
Peace is never a long, tall, elegant thing,

War, on the other boot, is always reappearing,
A grimy old fart, who never shaves too close,
Stumbles, and always turns up late,
For the very last beer on the very last boat.

And that dawn you could smell it, ionized,
War it was—and not with sea, no—

He snarled from the plastic palm behind the telephone,
Swung from the curtain like Tarzan

Along the bedroom rafters
As CNN broke the news.

He stalked me with those jellybean eyes,
This Quasimodo, his long tail flicking
Whip-like and the grim delight of his two front teeth
Sneering, ready to fight tooth and tear for apple.

My apple—a little round red thing
With sincere compliments from the General Manager.

All I had to fight back was a towel and a shoe.
At half-past five I surrendered.

Girl on the Corner of Chang'An Street

In those days I knew nothing, and you, you knew it all.
We could see it in the way you blinked.
And we all wished we had one like you.

Or the way you paused before you delivered your line:
You had them all down; all the way to the Rs
that hung there, baited, for big fish.

It made all of us think you were far smarter,
miles ahead, a sublime creature from a distant star.
You couldn't put a word wrong.

Over beers and Japanese cocktail snacks
they jostled and ruffled and prodded me, and the more I denied,
the more they believed it was true.

I let them simmer, bubble, thoughts popping,
so everyone who was anyone could see I had you
where you were soft and moist.

And without a word from me, somehow you played along:
winking in the corridor so they could see,
thrumming your polish-perfect nails.

Or sweeping back your hair, so they could catch a glimpse
of your ears, the ones they thought I had nibbled
on sweltering Beijing nights

when the maintenance man never came.
And once, when I saw you eating watermelon,
with your friend, crouched low on a street stall,

your skirt hitched all the way up to your knees,
I glimpsed the inside of your thighs,
the melon juice running down your chin,

and you, you, spitting seeds and bits of rind,
where fish heads and spines
lay rotting amongst flies.

Seepage

& when you Piotr stared at me unflinching point blank
offered me a malt whiskey with or without a splash
your wife puckering new lips on champagne

said it's all leaching under the foundations
can't let the shareholders know or the factory would close
I just smiled back & cheered our good health—

The world was big & cancer was everywhere
in the meat, in the bread, the sky, the unflinching earth
only in Iceland will the volcanoes get you

& then there was factory kingpin Ying
with the blue phone glued to his ear—
he who rose from the communist earth

he who bought a house for his father
then down the line all the way to his second
no, third, cousin, uncle to his sister's second half-brother

& thus it was, came to be
that effluents surpassed basic constituents to life
Jupiter coming out of the other end of the tap

leaking like an old man's dribble
in his dirty underpants
& you both said

by the time anyone noticed you'd be retired
enjoying life, a garden of herbs & flowers
good food somewhere on a Pacific island

with parrots & deep sea swordfish &
clear blue cloudless skies
until the final day of passing

That night I was all fuzzy on vodka
as a girl with watermelon breasts
screwed me almost half to death

Monkey Brains

We ate monkey brains in secrecy
just to see what they tasted like,
as if they might remind us of you;
and although the ancient custom
was to strap the chosen primate
in a made-for-measure cabinet
with only the shaved cranium exposed,
crush the skull-bone with a golden hammer,
while she screamed and whimpered,
begging for the beginning of time;
an experience, I've been told, like no other,
we preferred them fried in garlic and onions
separated from the body,
dipped them in rice wine vinegar.
You got sick after that, struggled
for ten days and nights,
dampening the sheets with your toxins.
I knew you'd live.
You wanted to die.
I remember the morning your fever broke
was the morning the H5N1 virus
flamed across the country,
everyone was wearing a blue mask
and we no longer feared the secret police.

A Revolutionary Commander Addresses His Troops

And so to war again to crush
those rabble-rousers. As the General

has often said, there's always another.
Discontentment must be flushed out—

extinguished like the red foxes
chattering beneath the bridge.

The good General, bless him, might,
in all his mercy, forget—when jocular

and jovial among brass bands and streamers—
that it serves no great purpose

to feed the living when they've
already been pronounced stone dead.

Why Yang Wants to Leave Wolf Mountain

(1)

Fused at birth, conjoined in skin & mind, I am but one
of the two likely unlikely, identical but for a green hue

settling behind my curious eyes and a black mole growing
under Yang's sensitive nose—Yang bears it as her symbol

of reason, I know it to be our mark of fate: an accumulation
of past lives rolled into one black F-sharp: the fortune-teller's

swansong. Mother tells us we arrived early in spring,
when wives sew first seeds under a waxing sun, that same day

the black-necked cranes return trumpeting over Wolf Mountain
to dance for eggs, to sing monogamous summer love songs.

(2)

And Yang and I become the double-entendre of all Wu county,
that staccato at the end of a Peking opera played on fields of barley—

an embarrassment for those with no faith, but a miraculous creation
for those who worship the salacious Buddha with the pot belly

like faithful Grandpa Ye who Mother says is incorrigible.
Evenings when he sips dragon brew from his chipped red cup

he chortles in our ears—in those days we have only one little Red
Book—but he sits there plunked on the edge of our bed,
            stomping

to scare off night mice, to ease us into our dreams with ancient tales
of villagers passing through winter's cold fingers, of fading

into the soft-snow of god-sky, only to remerge
as black-necked cranes under our mountain's early haze.

(3)

Grandpa Ye claims he knows each crane by name,
every unique swell and swagger, each bellow and grunt;

who flutters brazen like Great Auntie Ma or sways
on one leg like Great-grandmother Shie, and he jests

that Uncle Fu always gobbled too many fried dumplings,
croaked & ruffled his wings in a huff, but just like any crane,

deeply admired the round paleness of our spring moon
over Wolf Mountain; perhaps because it reminded him

of the crisp butter pancakes Auntie Ma would roast
on freezing winter nights, stuffed with scallions,

raisins and that secret recipe of hers for sticky brown rice.

(4)

On Father's behest when we turn eleven, Ah Yi Liu,
the midwife, slices us clear of each other, leaving a dragon

from armpit to hip, a squiggle so sharp it shimmers
like aqueous glass. Yang is walking alone among stems of barley,

between the daffodils within hours. I fever through pulsing
candlelight, in the arms of Mother and Ah Yi Liu

whose poultice of puerile sweet peppers and grasshoppers
brings me back as from the ancestors—who as I recall,

are so full of gossip and chatter they float gassed-up like balloons
amongst the clouds, swirling in formation like plump swallows.

(5)

Father sets off on horseback for the grand city of Chengdu
with its brocades and teas and its operas to negotiate a dowry.

His plan: to marry us to two brothers, eldest sons of Quartermaster
Chiu, a crocodile of a man who sails a junk down the Yangtze
       delivering flour

and salt berth-side to berth-side; for all portents Crocodile Chiu
has enough cash to bankroll all of Wu county. But Yang wants nothing

to do with young Sichuan rivermen and begins to consider her own plan:
A karaoke bar in the old alleys of Shanghai, she whispers one night.

She mentions something of Chairman Deng's song to getting rich.
Glorious, she says, all the glorious foreigner men, she says, muscles

like supermen, manners like lords and ancient kings. Would you
believe, they open doors for ladies and walk behind? she says almost
       unbelieving—

and all their delicious foreign cash, strapping men who would shower
us in blown kisses and Tequila Sunrise and jewels and jade and gold.

(6)

But as teenagers, when spring unfolds in its brighter colors
and as the sun and the black-necked cranes circle the skies,

Grandpa Ye once again begins his own little inside business,
drying leaf and shell and scraps of hide on the roof of our pigsty;

he burnishes snakeskin, batwing, bird-bone and carrot peel, coarse
goat straw and whatever else he can skim from less obvious surfaces.

And when the wind blows East, he bumps his brakeless bike
down the crooked path of the mountain, descends into valley below

where he rows out his old fishing boat—if you can call it that—
for it's patched with tar and peat and crane feathers.

It can only float for half an hour at most, but in that time
he nets dragonfly nymphs and flies and river lice; and all the fish

he happily tosses back, sluices down the river to the distant lands
of the Gongxian Bo, a people known for their brooding fishy ways.

(7)

And in the autumn he blends his dried mush mix, squeezes
it into tight bricks. And the men arrive eagerly on their pack animals,

on their mules and donkeys and yaks with salt and sugar and
green tea; and some even pay him in crisp red banknotes

far more than it is worth. They say it is the best smoking tobacco
money can buy and they hunger for its earthy mountain flavors,

so much so, that many puff pipe after pipe right here outside
our foul-smelling pig sty, among mud and hens and mice and

they stare longingly up at Wolf Mountain in wild abandon, where
birds swirl in mad clusters, and for a moment, entirely forget their wives.

(8)

Grandpa Ye knows that one day Yang and I will leave.
He tells me secretly he's seen Sister Yang in a dream,

running the great city from behind her hand-carved
sandalwood desk. And he says we will both become rich

beyond our young imaginations, beyond the landlords
of the imperial times, and when we'd leave the Mountain

we'd never return. I thought then that Grandpa Ye was prone
to embellishment, after all, he was a tobacco salesman,

but what little I knew, Yang had long ago mastered,
in that singular mole she so prized—under her twinned nose.

II

Paper Tigers

We shall support whatever the enemy opposes
and oppose whatever the enemy supports.

—*Mao Zedong*

Unseen

Huashan Mountain, 1843

I asked the Master
while he sipped his chrysanthemum tea

why after three years of study
I had still not encountered a god—

his churlish answer was one
that did not amaze—

it had nothing to do with my dedication,
nor the time that had elapsed

between the shuffle of the moon and the sun;
apparently, it had everything to do with my head.

To yearn for something he said
is simply not enough.

And then he smiled, and the sun
touched the mountain quite silently.

Red Omen

When I was fourteen, breathing white fire,
a comet blazed over the Taklimakan.

It slewed across the skies and flickered
red before it died.

                We knew dragons
had laid clutches here when
desert was blooming grassland.

And sometimes, we'd dig up scorpions' nests
and find shards of melon-sized dragons' eggs beneath.

One morning a sandstorm bellowed in our grotto
and they came with trucks and boots and black batons
slapping against their thighs.

They told our parents
we'd been getting things wrong for centuries.

They scolded, shook heads, raised voices, waved guns.

It was time, they said, to bring us children back
to a modernizing world.

And so, wrapped
under sheets of shifting stars,
we journeyed over mountains,
across plains, through valleys and villages, until

we entered the crystal city where there is no silence
and a thousand faces scrutinized us down to our teeth.

And they spun metallic around a red star upon a large square
like birds flocking around a magnetic tree.

That first night it was biting cold and we slept
in a hospital-sized house.
Yet, beneath my blanket,

pressed against my bony chest,

those shards of melon-sized eggshell,

warmed me.

Factory Girl

I've been told one of my girls in the factory has only just turned fifteen.
    My gut reaction is to fire her.

We've a responsibility to uphold the law and not just for the sake
    of the shareholders,

who'd throw a fit if the stocks dropped and our customers who audit us
    like dogs sniffing out a particular kind of trash.

Yet my factory manager with the toothy smile says we'd run a big risk
    of her blowing the whistle.

Her parents are dirt-poor farmers and can't even read; they live
    two thousand miles away on the edge of the desert wind.

"And what do they farm?"
    "Sand dunes." I can hear the toothpick lodged in his cheek.

Apparently it takes them half a day with a donkey
    to lug a bucket of water up the canyon.

"And what of school? If she doesn't work, who's going to pay for her books?
    her clothes? her knee socks?"

I consider this late at night after my teenage mistress has fallen asleep.
    Next morning I call my guy with the toothy smile.

But it's too late. She's caught a whiff.
    "Not to worry," he says—and I can hear his thin smile on the line—

"She's pretty, she's smart. She'll make some manager
    a good little wife."

Bicycle

They say I have a face like a bicycle
              & I wonder if from the front or the side

I guess it's a compliment since they ride them
              along the canal when the sun settles & the crane flies

Sometimes I watch the men soldiering home
              as if they've been to a wedding they've never had

trailing ribbons of paper from the burn of the machine
              & on the women from workshop number nine

plastic confetti sprinkled in their hair
              like tiny little confessions floating behind

One of our small perks is the after-shift dinners
              boiled rice & bok choy & dry fish heads

which my HR lady tells me is far better
              than what they normally get

              but little do I know, I'm merely transposed:
a colon sent from the board to point the way ahead

In nine solid months and forty-five thousand fish heads
              we've reached all targets; we've outperformed

        Kim Yung Boiled Meat Sticks
        Emperor Wu's Golden Fish Cakes

              Yes, indeed it's a miracle. The trick, of course
is in the distribution & getting them to appreciate

that only milk from free-range Western cows
            could settle the stomach of the Chinese working man

            could enrich the Ch'i so early in the morning
could steady the hands on the lathe

&, above all, making it available on bicycle carts
            outside every single factory in every single province

            Cream of Feng Shui
            Awaken the Tiger Within

            A yoghurt for the enlightened
            Free Range, healthy and keeps you slim

            & I wonder, as my term comes to an end, as I sit here
listening to each section manager praising my achievements

& the flowers & the toasts at the banquet table
            what they will think of the next face

            whether they will see him
as a traffic light or a conveyor belt

or a chair
            or even a cart

Crystal Casket

She, sweet pigtailed revolutionary
clenches sweaty palms, maypole dances stars
hopscotch hops cracks as banners thwap attention

salutes, then warbles red like the rest

shakes out the cold in padded peasant shoes.

He, man of the world, endures cockeyed stares
wide-eyed grins as the apple boxes spin
on the carousel at Capitol Airport

babies are stifled silent & velvet drapes mildew as they nip, sip, lip

subversive secrets flutter in the Friendship Hotel, locking fingers.

She, sweet pigtailed revolutionary
would die for jasmine tea; he, man of the world
would murder for filter coffee

Kung Pao liquor stinks 60 proof from every damn pore
early in the morning

Starbucks yawns wide behind the knobbed doors of heaven.

He, man of the world, clenches her sweaty palm
& the rest glare in the queue to see the sun-drenched sleeping king
peony petals scatter the ancient crystal casket

but the king smirks angelic, ennobled

vacuum-sealed, embalmed, death defying.

Wing Lu's Electromagnetic Repair Shop

Corner of Xinhua and Liaoningang Street, Zufu District,
Hebei Province, 1997

Car's being hammered.
Meteoritic clumps clang it back into driving shape.

We've never seen technique like this applied before
& a crowd gathers, rolling in on foot, bicycle, on the backs of trucks

the only thing missing is a stream of multicolored kites,
a marching band piping hot brass on the breeze.

Fireworks rattle in relay
somewhere beyond dimly lit grease & slick,

announce the feng shui of day turning night.
Old men spit & children spin wheel spokes grumbling asphalt.

Behind, a creek trickles
& it's put to good use testing flat tires, flutters

in plastic wrappers & bits of old boot.
Three boys in gray overalls like chimney sweeps or coal miners

burp & grunt like they're testing the resonance of steel against primal voice;
from a distance it almost looks like they've discovered a way of talking
        to matter.

We leave them & the harangue
(this will take its precious time, & such concentration costs).

We round the corner, reach the main road into town
where soiled tractors & other dusty three-wheeled contraptions

hold fast in rush hour, clunking, coughing thick black muck.
You can almost feel stomachs growling, shaking through

traffic lights pulsing. It's way past dinnertime;
on each side of the road single-celled-restaurants

lit bare in single light bulbs wave for trade, beckoning
savory fragrances of fried rice, spring onions & peanut.

A long line of women, young & old, queuing for a shop
catches the eye. Here something's alive. All the others are empty vying.

This place is not for grub, it looks almost medicinal,
a grand placard of a palm, beneath some scrawl,

holds out flat in Buddhist contempt.
(Or is it just to bless those patient in line?)

A blue curtain hangs in bay windows, sagging,
dragged down by dead weight, snatches of dim light

disco-throb inside; someone's deep in conference, holds up a chicken live,
perhaps to sacrifice; we hanker in, beyond respectful distance.

Woman beside us sighs, one in front mumbles a curse,
one has a snake & a crab in a cage, the other a clear plastic bag

with three fish lost in space; a third exits beaming ear to ear.
Woman at the front says, *Well? What did he say?*

Through the crack in the open door, we see inside,
& a man with a cleaver whacks off the chicken's head,

upends the body draining the blood
into a heavy metal bowl.

The victim cannot control her joy, covers her smile with her hand.
He said my son will be rich, a man among men, will rise the ranks,

until he becomes a Commissioner of Police in Shanghai.
Oh I am blessed, blessed by the gods. A good day to be alive.

Sometimes Someone Votes No, but I've Never Seen It

Lu Hua Farming Collective No. 5, Gansu, 2005

we vote green

if we agree

and red

if we don't

it's all

tallied up

by that man

over there

(with the square glasses)

churned evenly

in a clear plastic pot

so all can see

there can't be

any manipulation

of any kind

what could be more

democratic than that?

The Cult of Mother-Self

I must find out which is right, the world, or I.
—Comrade Jiang Ching (better known as Madame Mao)

19.00, Wednesday, Great Hall of the People, Beijing, 1972

      She points at the ceiling.

Everything's being recorded.
You'll receive a full transcript by tomorrow.
It'll be almost as if you had written it yourself.

This must be told for all women
and know, this is no work of fiction.

Discard what you may have heard,
my parents were rice farmers,
worked for the local landholder, a brute named Chiang.

He chained his daughters to trees for he believed
birdsong and shade were good for pale complexions.
And, of course, he couldn't have them running away
with hot-tempered farmer boys.

When I reached my teens I knew it was my destiny
to be a soldier of the common people,
to create the greatest equality of wealth in any land, ever;

and in the words of the great Karl Marx, 'To live for the people.'
and so, without my parents knowledge, I walked to the caves
of Yan'an where the people's movement all began—and somehow,
like all young women, I met a man, and fell in love.

He was far older than I, not handsome, but full of the power of nature
and the wisdom of the ancients. He was a poet and a revolutionary,
and he would change the world forever. I was his fourth wife, you know;

but I didn't mind. I would have been happy as his fifth or six.
But soon, I realized I had to find a way to do my part.
What did I know, dance, music, acting, art?

So I decided to make plays, songs with his words, later even movies,
To show the people what they had, what they could have:
The culture of the love of the father to his children.
And one day I became Mother, the queen bee,
the icon of the feminine revolution.

And listen, I'll tell you a secret.
Nothing has changed. They, they are all just warlords,
while He Zizhen was alive I was first concubine,
now I am Empress, soon to be dowager.

I would have been a man as my father wanted
and if the gods would let me.
As it turned out, in my later life, I took on the role of a man.

In the Ibsen play, *The Doll's House*, I was Nora,
who as you may know is silly and immature in the first act,
but becomes a mature woman transformed by the last.

I would not spell things out loud, but life teaches you things,
hard lessons, which make you who you become.
Look at me now. Who would have guessed
I would become an icon when I was born?
Certainly not my rice-farming father—even to my Mother Duck.

And you know Ibsen was a Norwegian, a stoic race admired
by that silly man, Adolf Hitler. And like my Chairman,
a man never to fall from grace.

15.15, Thursday, Yellow Pavilion, Kunming Park, Beijing, 1972

I have become that which I needed to become
in order to fulfill the destiny of our people.
Chosen or not is not really the question—
does anyone really have choice?—no, *become*—
become is a word I like.

It is a burden, you know. To be a mother to millions.
Children need Father, but Mother too.
Shall I become your mother?

I see you shake your head. No, not your maternal mother,
your real mother.

One who helps you grow into a responsible adult.

　　　　She waves her fan like a magic wand.

A Potential Foreign Investor Audits
the Red Star Hotel

Kunlun, 1994

*Somebody wants to take away the hammer and sickle from our flag and
replace them with a computer and satellite.*
—Deng Xiaoping

Above the reception, Mao looms all-seeing—
and with him Marx, askew,

his thick, mottled beard collecting cobwebs, muted
by decades of dark brown dust.

There's a theatre here, where once banners ran high
with yellow calligraphy on red, and a velveteen music hall,
an old five-piece drum kit and a Stravinsky cello poised on the stage.

You can still hear *"Sailing the Seas Depends on the Chairman"*
rumbling, as you recline in rosewood seats in the galleries—and
the snap and rustle of five flags on the wind, as poets and teachers in
dunce hats are bawling.

The hotel brochure also shows a bowling alley with ninepins
brimming nightly with bubbling youth, and a regulation snooker table
once shipped from salty Aberdeen, a gift for comrades in arms:
the Scottish Coalminers' Socialist Association.

This foyer could house the entire People's Liberation Army,
it spreads in all directions in pink-veined marble, they tell me,
imported from the shores of Baikal—and pink, not to hide
the blood of torture, but the liquids of unrequited loves.

Now, it's mostly hen-pecked cadres, retired army majors
that slip in the occasional nibble with pigtailed peasant girls

who thresh corn in summer but massage in winter:
Ayis with a taste for Italian shoes.

And then, there's the stir-fried hippies with lashings of I-Ching
who've scoured the country seeking the remnants
of a lost land: the Shangri La of Kunlun,
where far beyond the prayer-strewn passes, pyramids,
like those that house Tutankhamun, hold ancient wisdom.

They've been caught here.
Hovering.
On the internet.

The Chairman's Last Supper

Though
I taught
you how to fish the moon and stars,
drag them closer to earth, know this:
There's
always
a Judas
lurking
in the
shadows.
Let me
teach
you one
last thing
before
I make
my
grand
exit:
After
eating
all the
grassroots
and the
tree bark,
eat the soil.

Barbers

Ban Ban Soup Shop, Snake Head Alley, Nanjing, 1995

In 1915 I carted
combs, scissors, razors, clippers,
ear-cleaners & brilliantine in slippers.
In autumn, this same alley
was littered with hair
& leaves & chicken bone.

We barbers had a monopoly
on the head business
in the good old days.

If you weren't sporting
a Manchu queue
we'd report you,
& off with your offending head.

Now barber shops line
alleys from Harbin to Shentou,
& red & white candy poles
make you dizzy;
& to truck drivers, salesmen,
sailors, chancellors
on the fly
country girls offer quick head
with one hand on a tube
of Johnson's baby oil.

But enough chit-chat.
Let me finish my chicken soup.

Building a Japanese Butterfly

Descartes
was convinced
that each organ
was like a cog
or a wheel;
surely he knew
that the word

Organ

came from
the Greek
word for tool.
Strange the way
words evolve
into something
quite different
to that which
they were once

Intended.

Perceptions
and intentions
are quite often
at cross purposes.

Take my friend
Yamasaki:
he yearned
to build

the perfect butterfly

with circuits
spokes and rods.
These things too
are entirely

Organic.

Happy Hour at the Surrogate Bar & Grill

Shanghai, Saturday, 6:00 p.m., January 13, 1989

Mitsue tells me everywhere there are powerful vortices,
traps, pitfalls, invisible to the human eye,

perceptible to only the most intuitive souls.
These rifts have the ability to transform

Hitlers into Einsteins,
de Sades into Wittgensteins.

But she possesses a device she calls her VFP,
the Vortex Field Paralyzer, which, she says, helps her

sense ley lines, that she may tread
a single-minded path to a sensible end-goal.

She tells me it's no coincidence she was born an heiress
and that her natural curiosity for the unexpected

is a gift from a long line of ancient Okinawan ancestors.
After many years of scouring hidden places,

the jungles of Brazil, tin traps of Africa,
great mountain ranges of unknown lands,

over the great plains of Siberia,
she finally found the man, who by virtue

of his third eye and his fifth and eighteenth life,
gave her the key to build her VFP.

And with her millions and her legacy of intuition,
she has thrived well into middle age.

Mitsue flags down the bartender, orders another
round, then tells me under no uncertain circumstances

should I walk home alone tonight.
In Japanese, she says, Mitsue means *Branch of Light*.

The Smell of an Elevator

I've never known an elevator
to stink so much of garlic.

It must be Mister Huang
who's always farting

on the way to work.
Perhaps I should have a chat

with his good wife;
though, they say

she's a good cook
and you know

how good cooks are
about taking advice.

The Five Cantos of Canton Fair

Chinese Export Commodities Fair, Guangzhou, Autumn 2005

(Canto I)
Fair Love, & War

Like many ancient tea ports
Canton & its bi-annual extramarital affair

is about fine lines, cheap poker lust
swagger come bust, staring heaven-bent

high-rattling low hell-sent, balls on the table
knock-knock—

& two whole gun barrel cityscapes, tagged,
tucked & nipped by post-structural architects

in the click-clack of old Amsterdam gone guano,
woozy on dodged taxes,

spitballing reams of buttered contracts rubber-stamped
by ribbon-snipping politicians

& bomb-diffusing state-owned enterprises
with positive cash flow injections:

a hundred thousand fungi, a million sand snakes
puffed up & ready to strike.

China's sister cities to Heidelberg, Salzburg
& Kyoto sport matching wedding rings,

state-of-the-art perfect-teeth grins
of model hedgerow apartment complexes

miles deep cultivated like oyster farms,
then, roll in the hay

& swear sweet fidelity
to the very last kiss.

(Canto II)
Triple Moxibustion Ecclesiastic

Guangzhou, once Britain's opium-den,
with skies cataracting dim outlines
of prefab morning light,
rattlesnakes deep on the inside, intent
on winning back every penny it ever spent.

Behind banners in steel cages,
men & madams in folding picnic seats tout Inuit sealskin,
nickel-dipped brass plumbing sprockets,
Korean carbide, Brazilian titanium,
Australian iridium, and mother-of-pearl buttons
carved from deep sea Filipino oysters
fished hand to hand, daughter to daughter,
Indian cardamom & allspice vacuum-packed in Shenzen;
wicker baskets hand-woven by little women
with little children's fingers in Himalayan altitudes
(because only the small can wheedle
and too much oxygen makes you spin abstractions)
& tea cozies embroidered in turbans & minarets;
clear acrylic toilet seats prickling with fakirs' nails
& striking flush handles molded like hooded cobras,

Russian translators hanging Cyrillic signs which you think read:

Help me. I need buy ticket home,

but actually say, *Sino-Russian trade consultant ready to translate for all your business needs. Reasonable. Pay by hour.*

& Rolexed Mongolian princes hover near the gents beside ice cream
wagons where hot-dog stands with New York Relish &
penny-nipple girls with torsos for bending
backwards while whirling on rubber-tire swings.

There's nothing left for sale unless it's dead blown cold.

Cross yourself with holy water, duck, &—

Ching ching.

(Canto III)
Spruced Up, Served, & HIV Free
(Holiday Inn Shuttle Bus & Hall 8.1)

Dutchman Don on the bus tells me he exports blood
flash-frozen in South China to hospitals across the globe.
A, AB, O, plus & minus; it flows freely here,
along silt & slime & single-storied homes
where lakes have turned septic, emulsify bones.
Why let all the mosquitoes get it free of charge?
Five containers every month packed in vials, sterilized,
tested & tried by the caseload, by the pallet, or:
bloody well temperature-controlled, container-wise.

Wide-eyed Mack, over coffee near the gents
where a Mongolian prince is giving us the all-knowing,
tells me he's about to buy all the tousled hair
in Guangzhou; not for plugging movie producers in LA,
nor the wisp & weave of old-school chiffoniers in Hebron;
no, instead of yeast for raising pre-packed, centimeter-sliced bread.
It's all in the head, he says, *all in the head*. Mack's an Aussie,
baker turned buyer, a real Pillsbury high-flyer. Apparently hair,
melted down, works just as well as eukaryotic micro-organisms.
Hair, you see, is just a kind of human fungus,
possibly schizosaccharomycetic.

At least, that's what Mack says, back-hand pressing his card on
a Russian gal in a tight white cardigan with a name tag that reads:

Ask me. I'm here to help.

(Canto IV)
Teddy Love

Down aisle 14-3, stall 54,
between Nanchung Ladies Undergarments I/E
& Cixi Standard Screwing Parts,
Teddy Al'Huk Salami, also known as Teddy Love,
Lagos-born, China-studied, fingers me in.

Sign above reads:

Teddy's Love Machine Incorporated: Exporter of teddy bears & other
fuzzy love.

In his perfect, white-teethed Mandarin, between 100% cotton t-shirts
with sparkly hearts & *I Luv Manhattan,* Teddy smokes Cubans,
Butterflies just like Fidel, flogging mostly to Cameroon, Benin, Namibia,
Mauritius & a little fine crockery trade with the Isle of Man
where cousin Hassan has a Chinese restaurant called The Hot Wok Pot.

'S all diced up, Man, he says running a long comb through his hair like
he's trying to ruffle up a threadbare carpet, then leaves the comb
standing there, upright.

*Any deal you can get, I can get it better. I'm Da Nigerian MC of
Canton Love.*

Teddy buys me a beer over lunch, some kind of seafood stew, mussels,
clams & spiny sea cucumbers, popping up for air. In less than five
I'm running like the clappers for the loo.

& later, when dim haze becomes black Canton night, Teddy shows me sights.

Narrow Chinese eyes don't see no African shadows, he says. *Only
neon lights.*

All-Jamaican Tijuana Brass Band at the Buddha Bar plays Herb Alpert.

Here Teddy keeps a wicker rocking chair—I've seen them at the fair,
& rolls spliffs, bags out Skank & Twist & White-Haired Lady until dawn
making fine use of the disco lights of Dewberry's next door to confuse
the cops.

Who, as Teddy says, *can't tell a Torpedo from a full-on fag.*

(Canto V)
Blood Brothers

Three a.m. at Dewberry's, they're all icing up:

Don the trader-vampire, Mack the buyer-baker, & Teddy, upended &
ready to roar.

Don's wining a Thai transsexual & doesn't have a clue
that she sports something honest & straight between the legs.
Mack's dancing with a midget of a woman,
his hands all a-flutter, & Teddy
has two Ukrainian blondes with straight-ahead boobs
like a pair of old-fashioned pots for sugar cubes.

Teddy's wired, he says, on life, since he'd never hisself
touch any of that Rainy Day Woman he bags out back.

The Russian birds are on temporary loan from a Mongolian prince
No. 5, Teddy's groovy deed to the antecedents of Genghis's loins.
To him they're all crown jewels, especially peroxide, but best on the run.

& somehow morning rolls on, chickens are laying.

Teddy says, *Tell me anything you like. But whatever ya say, China,
Africa, friggin' coconuts & rice. You know, in the end it's all just blood.*

Four a.m. at Dewberry's & the crowd whittles down to narrow bone:

Mack's lost the knead in his baker's hands & Don's gone home alone.
Delicious Candy from Mauritius materializes with a flip-back notepad
& a pink marbleized fountain pen (they sell for thirty out back, off the
rack).

My head is whirling on shots of pink blaze, Guangzhou daze.

Candy hands me the thing, it reads:

*This contract is made in two copies and in accordance with the
laws prescribed by the Geneva Convention and mutual goodwill
and consent, regulated by the rules and regulations of the People's
Republic of China, and shall be considered fully binding and valid
on all counts for the duration of the contract and is signed with the
goodwill of both parties.*

Or something like that. Amen.

Moonlight Bebop

The Peace Hotel, Shanghai, 1993

The old jazz band plays for hard cash, bills in advance,
song by lonesome song. Hotel guests read laminated
grease-flecked menus alongside manhattans and martinis

poured with abandon under a light glow
of flickering fluorescence trying to recall
Louis Armstrong's *Wonderful World*, in between pumped-up

cheeks of trumpet, *The Girl from Ipanema* where Mister Piano
shakes maracas, or *As Time Goes By*, softly croons
'You must LEE-member dis...' Dirk and Ingrid

shanghaied, toe to toe, eye to eye in the gloom.
Bar smells faintly of damp linoleum and cocktail onions
and when *In the Mood* swings in, clarinet on solo,

the tempo is a hitch too slow, warbling in E-flat.
There's a bird chirping in the rafters
and our waiter's going at it with a wet mop to the tune of

Bridge Over Troubled Water.
This is Mister Ren, our bandleader's,
favorite. Every time he ends in tears.

It reminds him of his first wife, Lu Lu,
who plunged into the sludge of the Yangtze
from the tallest bridge in town so she could admire the view.

Billy the drummer hunches over his kit.
He's about to tumble in himself;
really he's falling asleep; only his wrists flick and snap

as if someone just wound up his spring.
Soon I think his teeth will start chattering castanets;
sure enough, someone's paying for *Nights in Spanish Harlem*.

And when we get up to the room, undressed,
laid bare to foggy Shanghai moonlight
and all the rosewood is staring wide-eyed,

you look like much like a wilted rose, red gone deep plum.
Somewhere I hear *Chattanooga Choo Choo*—
it's Mister Ren in falsetto;

and you stand at the window taking in the air
that smells like fish and gasoline and wonton soup.

The Analects of Wu Wei: *Virtuous Dog Meat*

The Master said, 'The virtue embodied in the doctrine of the Mean is of the
highest order. But it has long been rare among people …'
— Doctrine of the Mean, The Four Books (300 B.C.?)

There's a farm on the outskirts of Beijing
that abuts a stubborn goat of a restaurant

blooming in red paper lanterns
waitresses in gold flowing dragons.

It's right next to the butchery, who cleave
off the cuff, by sleight of inclined hand.

Observe the healthy twinkle, the saliva
frothing on the edges of their tongues

a healthy sheen like a courtesan's hair
brushed ninety-nine times each night

before moonlight, breeze, and sing-song.
And the breath, the breath must exude

a mild earthy whiff, much like cut hay
on balmy Hangzhou autumn winds

while overlooking West Lake, Xi Hu
which is always alluring among the lilies

and the three pools where dragonflies chatter.
And the tilt, the tilt of the head

is the sure bent of a curious mind
you will inherit, everything you devour

man, you see, is the alchemy of all his meals.
And the blood, the blood should be dark

tender red, fluttering just like her lips
under soft dawn-struck mornings.

They say it's good for all manner of ills,
Mutton of the Earth we call it

and it keeps you warmed, ready
to pierce and pinion while

the Eight Immortals of the Wine Cup
write reflections in fluid tippled verse.

*

More dog is a better for a boy
and better in the ninth month
on the ninth day, in the ninth hour.
          And dog and nine
are both pronounced 'Gau.'
For nine months it takes for a good child
to be released into the coils of old men.
          Dog, dog always
washes down well
with a dram of Shaoxing rice wine
and a daydream of Li Po drinking
          alone, heartens, sweetens.

*

A dog who dies in pain
is all the more
for its last breath.
And when you
devour its suffering
you thus absorb its heat.
        Ah yes,
it is far more reasonable
for a carnivore
to eat red meat.

Xiao Hong's Great Leap Forward

A clean sheet of paper has no blotches, and so the newest and most
beautiful pictures can be painted on it.
—*Mao Zedong*

Tradition says: Women are grass.
Tradition says: Women are born to be stepped on.

We burn our schools and books to the ground.
Teacher Liu looks like a stork in a dunce hat.
Red Guard Pang beats him silly with bamboo.

Chairman says: Brothers and sisters are equal.
Chairman says: Women uphold half the sky.

Hot fire is red, blood is red.
We don't need entertainment.
Our theater is played out on the streets.

Chairman says: Without destruction no construction.
Chairman says: Be red. Don't be an expert.

When I'm twenty-one I dance chest-to-chest
with Chairman in the park.
My heart leaps for joy, I nearly faint.

Chairman says: Melt hot steel in your back garden.
Chairman says: Stoke a furnace beneath your apple tree.

And we become scarecrows, we kill
the sparrows for our Great Helmsmen,
for they are the scourge of the fields.

Chairman says: Revolution is not a dinner party.
Chairman says: Make the future new!

Comrade Pang lights Chairman's Panda cigarette.
Up close he smells of lotus flowers.
I wish I could kiss him on the mouth.

Chairman says: He is the sun that never sets.
Chairman says: These are the best years of our lives.

And my heart grows
redder and redder and redder.

Iron Rice Bowl

Xi Fa Agricultural Commune No. 5, Xi Fa Village, Henan Province, 1999

Lao Po is pregnant again.
She can't get enough fried pork dumplings
and we daren't tell a soul.

Mrs. Wu from the Child Planning Centre
is here on Wednesday.
Lao Po will be sick in bed.

For three years after the birth
all Lao Po and I eat is rice porridge
with a sprinkle of salt.

We give away all our crops
to pay Mrs. Wu. Han Xing Guo cannot help it,
but she is only a girl.

We nearly starve to death
and Lao Po becomes chicken-thin.
The villagers joke the funeral man has two and a half coffins prepared.

Lucky for us, in the fourth year
our eldest comes home from Beijing.
He brings us fish and vegetables and noodle soup.

Oh, what luck to have a son!

Citizen Julius Wong

Fiji, 1999

Up the garden path
waving with his left
his right tucked
deep in his pocket
looking for a home.
He reminds me
of a pot of tea
an elephant
staring out to sea.
He jokes it ended diced
in someone's sausage
fried with onions.
Says all the blood
in his one good hand
has washed away
for good
in amends.
Julius is older than the sea, but then
he gives tomatoes new life
cucumbers
delicate ivies
exotic hyacinths
trawled serpentine
down the Amazon
to a little Chinese shaman
in the South Pacific
just like Gauguin.
They say he often dives
one-handed, tends corals
plays with parrot fish.
He paints seabreezes
when he isn't battling

aphids or having words
with the Prime Minister
on constitution or coup.
And halfway through
all the voice leaves his lungs
all the words leave his face
but he waves
beyond the waves
as if he truly meant it.

Tai C'hi Master

He has the humor of a freshwater trout.

        Speckled, he's nothing but sinew and bone

and what he calls pure elemental energy,

something he says is lethal unharnessed,

        just like the inevitable consequences

of Oppenheimer and uranium.

He maintains he can bring his vibrations

        right down to the dulcimer twang

of the universe,

and as the sweat pours off him

        he's doing the crane, spinning the globe,

one hand up, one down, into a hot roll.

Stacks and Smokes

There was never an end to the factories.

The more we stared, the more seemed to appear.

It was as if there were factories producing factories

And any imaginable thing could be forged,

Weft, cleft, stamped, ground, riveted—

In the end, something always had to be made,

And something else had to be made to make it.

Thick End of a Camel's Tail

Uyghur Halal Barbeque, Beijing, 2006

Gobi creeps into big cities
flecks under human nails

she has her way of smoothing things
down to the nature of themselves
her hard glass grain like blood-hungry mosquitoes

purple-haired housewives
in Saturday-starched window-shopping dresses

fit for an all-night & -day *Ganbei* wedding in fifteen pearl-embroidered
wedding gowns
& a dowry fit for a chairman

but when they finally stumble home
barefoot in the pitch

giggling like foxes
heels swinging
ribbons of cigarette smoke float
like ghostly Christian halos

& when the Bactrian camel snorts for summer
Mr. Hua is still cycling after all these years

he chews my tender lamb skewers
milk-fed on the Tarin Basin
(where Beijing's tested atom bombs)

he loves to hear himself humming revolutionary songs
above the wallop & squeal of Benz & Beemer

diesel gives his *shashlik* just the right atheist bite

he's pedaling to the Executive Council
behind banners & slogans & waves
to Ayi Lui with the peonies & roses & apple blossoms

as the lamb unfolds on his pointed tongue
he wipes his crystal-sewn eyes

& he stumbles into his conference hall
where he knows who wags for whom

Father's Milk

scribbled on the back of a napkin at the Nanning No. 2 Agricultural Commune 7th Annual Industrial Progress Festival, 1993

Once, we had the campaign
against bourgeois liberalization,

then, upside-down values
created economic reform.

A common prosperity
is the goal of our leaders:

Get rich quick,
but let some
get rich first.

Confucius said:

Even a journey of 1000 miles
begins with a single step.

III

One Hundred Flowers Bloom

Let a hundred flowers bloom;
let a hundred schools of thought contend.

—*Mao Zedong*

The Red Underpants

Well, they were just hanging there.
What else would you expect me to do?
especially when I'd known he'd worn them,

even more so when a breeze caught that lace edging
and it fluttered ever so lightly, and that image
came to mind—something I had seen

in an Attenborough documentary for the BBC.
It was some kind of weird-looking squid-creature
pulsing his tailwing against the black night of deep sea,

and he stared through the camera
right at me with his one single eye
and I swear he had a dirty look on his face

just like an Amsterdam-window-front-lady
enticing me into her plush boudoir.
Anyway, there they were, frilly and lacy and red,

and just caught with a dappling of breeze
so I slipped over the fence—there was no one at home—
stripped down to my buff and slipped them on.

O how they felt on my bare behind,
like angels caressing my cheeks
like heaven cupping my balls,

But just knowing I wore his underpants,
his frilly, red underpants, and knowing that somewhere
from far up on a rooftop, someone,

perhaps one his own bodyguards
was watching me through a pair of binoculars
made my spine tingle and my skin goosebump.

Broken Buddha

Jaipur, India, February, 2010

O, cracked-head, chipped-ear Buddha
can you still hear the winds of Samsara?

the seated, glowing bellies of immaculate men?
the wind-whipped dharma-spin of wheels

moving in coalescence with the planets?
Can you still feel the whip of ignorance?

The war of possessions?

O, cracked-head, chipped-ear Buddha
you've lost your right hand with its great 'O',

its A-OK, and you lean, top-heavy in the sand
remembering everything you never saw

your great eyes downcast on earth and acorns.
The priests here wish you to listen to their songs,

the immortal chants for all things living or once lived.

O, cracked-head, chipped-ear Buddha
do you see the elephant with the ragged ears

the drudge-child of chain and logs and common men,
those who carry fat Spaniards and Americans

up to the great fort on the hill as a monkey
sticks his finger in your chipped ear.

Do you still hear?

Still hear?

Hairy Crabs

In every pair of legs they have, the crabs are full of tender jade-like meat.
Each piece of ruddy fat, which in their shell bumps up, emits a fragrant smell.
Besides much meat, they have a greater relish for me still, eight feet as well.
—Cao Xueqin, Dream of the Red Chamber

Twelve nerve-wracking hours to Beijing, two more to Shanghai
& he finally eases into the tight skin of his Marlboro Lights.
In between hearty gulps, he rolls up his sleeves, then rustles out
contracts three miles long. He's poised above the dotted line

So where's the merchandise?

but they've laid on a banquet in his honor: a river of maidens
in ivory hairpins strum *pipas* & one-thousand-year-old eggs
pickled in horse urine, phoenix wrestling in swallows' nest soup,
lard-massaged warthog roasts on the bone & copper pots of jasmine

It's your factory, right?

piping hot in eight-scented wonders. But he grumbles, fogs up the van,
then points straight out the window, so they shuffle on
past fields of raw earth once flickering ripe in rice & pagodas,
knob upon knob of garlic & onion diced & sizzled

You know I need the lowest price

for gods, but now, fish-fed farmers in scruffy jumpers
cast iron, stamp steel & squeeze rubber under leaky tin roofs
& pallets nailed by three old boys a hammer & a padlock
stack higher than the looming spires of Our Lady of Lourdes.

But you can't neglect the quality.

Satisfied he's met the curator, he leans back to watch his smoke rise,
then a man in rubber gloves plates up hairy crab, an alien creature
spawned in liquids behind the factory, crawled to life under a full moon.
He ogles his chopsticks puffing & poking the furry claws,

The wife will never believe this in a million years.

after removing the top shell, the eyes, & sucking out the rich yellow roe,
the manager suggests he may use the carcass as an eco-friendly ashtray,
but he prays it will rear up & scuttle back downstream; meanwhile,
they've analyzed his prices & they're shaking their heads, wondering

Just look at the size of its claws.

why in the name of gods they rolled out of bed; still,
crab's on the menu, ambrosia of ancient kings, so they cock back,
shovel in, spitting & snorting & huffing in great delight & he mutters
Ave Marias incensed behind the haze of his Marlboro Lights.

Redshift Over Hunan

Southwest China Airlines Flight 204, 1995

Chinese New Year: floods abound and rain
is weft on the wing, Hunan lies waterlogged below,
paddies waist high. Tonight no one wears socks,

they're bailing for dear life, sandbagging.
Southwest China Airline pilots never announce,
never croon *seatbelts and upright tables*.

When we reach the rough and tumble of cloud-cover,
you close your eyes, imagine you're on a train
on the way to Hauptbahnhof. *Grosser Gott*.

Elena and the kids are waiting in Friedrichshafen
with Benni the Dachshund and the Blaupunkt.
You never know, it all might end in this turbulence,

in these drafts of pelting, zigzagging lights.
You are amazed, perhaps calmed to see
the man from Beijing next to you grog and slum,

his false teeth clinking into his coke
as our spacecraft rattles and surges
upon re-entry, buffeting the ozone.

I think know you're seeing your father-in-law
riddled with bullets of cancer, catheter on his knees.
A demise of Bavarian weeks—and a moment here, all for

lighting up sports cars on the cheap—vanished in storms,
vanquished in asylum: Yes, the first thing you'll do
when you reach Hong Kong, is to eat bratwurst

at the Hofbrauhaus down in Wanchai where Filipino waitresses
named Rosalie and Mariella and Prunella curtsey
and leave you their number on flimsy paper napkins.

Legs, Hands, Fingers,

Golden Dragon Textile Mill, Foshan, Guandong, 2005

Women uphold half the sky
—Mao Zedong

Her rejects on the production line
reach a new factory high.
QC Manager Pu has words:
'Concentrate, girl,' he says,
waving his pencil like a baton,
'You know you get paid by the piece.
At this rate you'll never be able to pay off your apartment,
go bowling with the girls.'

Somehow, Lu Xi has no more feeling
in her fingers
and she isn't much thinking about bowling.
'What you need is a good man,'
says her friend, Mai Dan.
'Does your mother
not push you to get married?'
Perhaps that's it,
thinks Lu Xi at lunch,
struggling to hold down her rice,
thumping her chest to quieten the bird inside.

Yet, there is something else that bothers her.
Something more than the bird.
It feels like a snake is squirming
inside her intestines. *Perhaps the bird*
is trying to eat the snake, she thinks.
But there is no explanation
for her legs, for her hands, for her fingers.

Swinging Swords in the Park

Jimmy Liu came with all the certs and five gold buttons.
In the first week the boy sold two thousand tons
to a little old man from Wuhan who nibbled
pumpkin seeds on the go.

Boss Wang gave Jimmy five cartons of Lucky Strikes
and a sweet cappuccino
frothing Starbucks.

And the boy puffed them all, inhaling
smoke and frost and dust rolling off the Gobi,
across the rooftops of the Forbidden City, watching
the sway of cherry blossoms
in the Summer Palace gardens.

But the poker-playing exiles sitting at table number 3
in the *Sichuan Lotus Garden* who slurped three bowls of noodles
in hot sauce, warned Boss Wang. They said:

Young Jimmy Liu is in the Falun Gong.
We've seen him swinging swords in the park,
lashing at authority in the air, would you believe?

They teach truthfulness, compassion and forbearance.

And Boss Wang abhorred non-profit institutions,
particularly those with bald,
lopsided or bearded men, and so he made the call.

And three members of the Party in black suits took the boy away
to the furthest corner of the nation
where elephants still roam the cloud forest
and monkeys gobble fruit from trees.

Word of Advice from Blue Moon Rising

Yantai, Shandong Province, 1999

The thing is, I've never considered
myself a businesswoman; just a tippler
of human emotion, a player of the
immaculate order, who knows how to
ply her hand at things that swell the tongue:
deep fried squid in fresh, iced batter;
diced chicken with roasted cashews,
steamed turtle, cooked in its own shell—
anything that tastes good with only
a marginal investment. And my clientele,
well, they're not what you call discerning,
I've tried all kinds of tests—watering down
the soup, substituting fresh onions with
only the skin, and you know, no one
notices a damn thing; so, my pockets
are heavier than I dare say, or show,
and the will to please is less of a thing
than a bare necessity, so I've studied
TV shows where emotions are on call
and listen to the trembling inflections
of old wives complaining about their
daughters on the radio, and I've mastered
the whole bing, bang and caboodle.
I'm what you call a master of deception.
So eat and be merry, sip and slurp
with my service with a smile, and
know one thing: it's all about how
you ply your trade, rather than how
it tastes. The basic rule is threefold:
cut, cut, cut, and when in doubt, cut again.

Genghis Khan in the Hot Seat

Hohhot, Inner Mongolia, 1992

Along the main drag of neverwhere,
streets are slick ice;
everyone slips, skates or bounds;
cars are like boats
and the Golden Horde Hotel, locked
in hot steam, is sweltering
at forty-five degrees;
sweater, parka, scarf, lie limp on the bar,
languid reflections of the bitter cold outside,
and the Qingdao beer comes in
a thick, frothy thirty.

Heavens above!
                              yelps the bedraggled bartender, plying
his flea-bitten moustache
with pointed thumb and fuck-you finger.

(He says his three-inch yellowed nail
is for scratching his wife's back.)

You shouldn't drink cold beer in winter!

Very bad for stomach.
Besides, hot water keeps out
all manner of evil ghosts.

Gerald Montague, in his three-piece herringbone, chuckles
like he just stepped out of the Raj.

He's the only Tai Pan far and wide, only he knows punch lines
of heavy smelters and coal mines.

Bartender Fu, a Manchu, buffs glasses to a fine glint,
then smiles a bridge of two false teeth.

All the steam makes everything glimmer.

Gerald sells machines that stitch leather
at the ends of the Earth.

I C E,
              he sighs poetically,
sipping Pushkin Vodka from Soviet-cut crystal glass.

This place has every other lollypop-licked—
even the sour plum of Pyongyang.

Believe me, I've tried.

Here ice,
              he says,
                            is metaphor for life: impossible to catch,
frozen in seconds, and evaporates in short winter light.

Yesterday, I skittered over the road to get some smokes,
but landed flat on my arse.

It's ten on a Sunday morning
and not a soul on the blank slate of the road.

Great Khan's tribe stares behind glass.

A little old lady steps out.
She's carrying a bent shoulder-pole
with two buckets of steaming dumplings.

Shuffling half-a-foot an hour.

Suddenly, a bus swings down the main drag.
No other traffic, not a blooming thing.

And you won't believe it, but this lone bus, slipping
in the direction of a camp for light crimes, skids,
then roars on its brakes—
                  a hubcap clatters,
                          dumplings roll towards the
gutter.

No one bats a lid. Not a single blink.

So enjoy your bloody beer:
it's warm and fuzzy and ice free here.

And Fu, turn up the heat!

Oh, by the way, the next one's on me.

                                      Fu fills me up.
                                      I shiver hot and cold.

A Model Enterprise

after a banner on the wall in a Shandong Cotton Mill, 1996

is ambidextrous, grips with all ten fingers,
set targets based on revolutionary peel.
The zest is the bite of an orange,
the all-seeing-eye, pips, a bittersweet offspring,
an offering to our Great Helmsman in the sky.
But, for heaven's sake don't spit them out.
Swallow them whole, feed them to birds.
We need to spread our seeds far and wide.

Bloodless (Why I Spend My Weeknights at the Silver Pig Karaoke Club)

Lao Lu at 2:00 a.m., after singing 'Save All Your Kisses for Me'
three times in a row

Xi Ban doesn't tickle no matter where you pinch or prod.
She cackles only at the inane: rabbits wrestled from banker's hats,
balmy, moonless nights that splutter warm rain,

and her giggle sounds like an asthmatic wheeze. Of all things,

she seems fascinated with facial quirks: noses twitching,
raised eyebrows, inflated nostrils, involuntary movement of ears.
For her, it's like observing primates at the zoo, and she's aware

of precisely when she's supposed to kick in.

And although this does provide some evidence that she really is
a form of living organism, to me she is made of cold
plastic tubes, wired with internal rubber joints that bend and give

like those ribbed industrial lubrication nozzles, positioning themselves

conveniently whichever way might be required to cool hot steel
while cutting, grinding or polishing quintessential mechanical parts:
cogs, spokes, wheels and shafts that turn, roll, spin and zigzag.

Mostly, I feel I am trying to shake her awake, re-start her engine

by rattling her like a faulty vending machine; then, and only then,
she smiles for a second: a stilted tweak of thin, dry lips. Xi Ban never
does anything just for the hell of it, on a whim or a wish
            or even a whisper.

All of her makes me want to drink Jack Daniels and croon
            Brotherhood of Man.

Suzie Lam Scorns the Happy Marriage Dating Agency

Toes

Twenty-something Suzie Lam, my dirty-weekend fling, tells me identity is a fickle thing, says everyone grows up wanting to be a cowboy or an astronaut, when all we really need is to cross a river without getting wet. Suzie wiggles her black-nail-polish toes and spoons herself Häagen-Dazs straight from the tub.

For some reason she likes to eat in bed.

Husbands

If you don't know who you are how can you go find a husband who can walk straight on two feet? When you want to grow up, you've got to shed your skin. Yes, I've become quite a snake she says, and hisses. In my case it was a shabby straw hat, parents who couldn't write or read and a cat named Ding Dong who was afraid of mice. In Szechuan everything trembles beneath your feet so there's nothing really to stand on. Hong Kong, on the other hand, is built on promises.

There's a dribble of ice cream on her chin and I'd love to lick it right off, only I know she wouldn't go for that.

Words

I used to keep a diary, all my history narrowed down to a thin disguise.
Now only what's still to come serves a purpose. At the dating agency,
there's no such thing as a happy marriage. Normally the men arrive
in a taxi, sometimes with a bunch of peonies, hair greased back into a
quiff. They know if I'm not interested; I just tell them let's just be friends
then. I've never finished a single date.

She licks her fingers, fluffs her pillow and stares at the fan on the ceiling.

Chatting

The QQ Chat Service is an excellent thing; the internet draws a higher
class of men. Most Chinese marriages are not built on love, you know,
but I'm not willing to compromise, not just yet.

Besides, I know you'd never leave your wife.

Revolution

Lin Biao in a note to Zhu En Lai, Hunan, 1949

The flower of China's youth
gather on the banks
of the Yellow River

Our new slogan:
If you have money give money
If you have a gun give a gun
If you are healthy

Come and fight

Repeat Customer

The Owl & The Pussycat, Wanchai, Hong Kong, 1999

I first met Suzie Lam in Wanchai where poles lit up
     in shiny bright girls. Her mama-san, an émigré herself—
born on the moldering banks of the Yellow River—
     once a carnival girl, a spinner of plates on bamboo poles

who travelled the length of Old Cathay to entertain
     Emperor Chiang's Kuo Min Tang, broke before
the happy revolution, inspired by Marx, Lenin, and Stalin.
     Mama-san, aka Liu Min Fan, often said, after sucking down

three or four watered-down gins, that she never understood
     the Chairman's fascination with all things Russian:
for one thing, they didn't have good food. And for that reason,
     and that reason alone, she refused all Russian girls

a twirl on the poles or the Guangdong lingerie
     of the *Owl and the Pussycat*. Suzie, on the other hand,
was like a daughter, and from the windswept mountains
     of Szechuan—where China grew its plumpest chilies.

She loved the word 'chilies'. Each visit, Mama-San,
     tried to convince me that Suzie would make an ideal wife;
not only was the girl schooled in rural domesticity
     ('just think of all the dust in those mountain villages,

but farmers' daughters know to make good soup from old bones.')
     Since arriving in Hong Kong, Suzie had learned English,
Japanese, Swedish massage, ('and would you look at that little body?
     Touched up by the most skilled surgeons: the blossoming lips,

the peachy nose, once-jug-handle ears now pink little oysters
     tucked behind her hair, all the excess removed.')
Mama-san was wiser than any Happy Valley racehorse trainer,
     and ensured that all her girls ate well, slept just enough

to keep their pale evening complexions, attended dance courses
     like rhumba and Argentine tango, knew how to sew buttons.
She, Mama-San said, was Auntie Liu, and for a small commission
     would ensure that in the end, each of her precious darlings

would find their lordly manors. And, as for me, as usual,
     there was a special discount. Anything for a repeat customer.

Madame Chao's Love Revolution

I say the Cultural Revolution
is the father of the sexual revolution
and the one-child-policy her mother.

Bet you didn't know that seventy percent
of the world's love toys
are made in southern China, did you?
Madame Xi down the street has a rose
that opens up into a pair of frilly panties
good enough to eat and a dildo that melts
in your mouth like dark Belgian chocolate.

But for the Chairman's sake,
don't spam your sex like Wu Lan.

They say she can be heard moaning
like all the way to Suzhou Creek.

And what ever happened to your Mao badge?
That suit that buttoned up to here?

I know, my Mother says:

My daughter is a whore...

But she thinks:

If the Cultural Revolution
were to come again, I would kill myself.

I'd rather my daughter be a whore
than a Red Guard.

Bend over.
I hear those foreign devils call it doggy style.

Driving for Goat

Country Roads, Hebei Province, 1995

I swear he can sleep while he's driving.
Or is it that he drives while he sleeps?
It doesn't matter, he gets there anyway,
strapped in as if he's ready to break the sound barrier.

His pinhole eyes let in just enough light
to see a straight fix ahead: This battered road
has felt the tread of so many tractors
it knows what it means to eat rubber.

Farmers no longer grind by hand,
millstone upon millstone;
they let the cars do all the work,
quickly swerving, chuffing up.

(Possibly there's enough corn here
in tire tread and tarmac to feed the Third World.)

Sometimes, he says, *a child gets in the way*,
between dried husks of corn,
jumping like pesky gnats, hovering,
running after rolling balls, spinning on bicycles.

Sometimes letting stones fly
they lose an arm or a leg.
You have to watch how you go, he says.
Last time, I hit someone's prize goat.

What did you do? I ask, observing a little
boy trying to fly a kite from a roof.
Do? Nothing, he says, going down on
the brakes, screeching to a halt.

A mother goose and her chicks cross.
I paid the farmer fifty Renminbi,
stopped at the next restaurant and ate
the best roast with five heads of garlic.

Now we're about to reach Lu Yuan,
the county of one thousand rams.
Someone shouts in the back:
Dibs on the balls!

Base Pairs

old Shanghai drags her feet
from screw-top jars
so she can avoid the bite
just to have a pee
comes in slow spurts
when taxis brim
with umbrellas
but buildings still rise
the elevator
never smiles
& your tea-leaves
the seventeenth floor
to cook a steamed fish!
for the pan to heat
the gas is always grumbling
of the hammer drill in apartment 1804
of Tibetan yaks up there
with their green & white bricks
they jostle & prod & poke
my, my you're fatter than ever, or
is your granddaughter still not married?
you're about to win again

sips hot tea
holds herself for hours
of the heartless bathroom
which anyway
on rainy days
men beat each other
senseless
& the woman who mans
with a flick of the switch
except when your grocery bags burst
spill all over
oh the trouble
the time it takes to wait
the water to bubble
& the thump & grind
sounds like a herd
at sunset Auntie & Uncle arrive
of Mahjiang
saying things like:
that's not your real hair color, is it? or
but you rub your hands together
& soon there will be all this

Pea Soup

Good Lord New Housing Development, Shanghai, 2005
—for Iris

We thread the last thin alleys of what this place
once has been: crumbling Art Deco, molding

Renaissance, Jewish ghettos, Russian dance halls—
fifty cents for half an hour with a Contessa.

It's all moving to dust, dying or infirm.
Glitter replaces stone. Tin replaces brick.

Wrappers, dirt, and flaps of rotting cabbage.
But there's a place the Realtor knows

that's just the lunchbox: All is not lost, he says.
There's romance here; pizzazz too.

Along the algae-stained canals where mosquitoes
flourish in cracks of asphalt and concrete

it rises low, expansive beyond the fish market,
where there are just as many flies

and a sweeping staircase flanked by Roman columns;
inside there are ballrooms and a botanical garden

where you can take the air under eaves of ivy.
Just you wait, he says, this is a treat for the eyes:

a restful island in a storm of honking horns, disguised.
This, dear friends, is a full knockout: stucco fountains,

Rococo, Grecian urns, and chandeliers with more crystal
than even Liberace's once-twiddling fingers,

Elvis Presley croons in velvet from the walls,
but the centerpiece in the marbled hallway

is the statue of a horse, rearing for charge,
and plonked right on its seat is Lord Wellington

saber raised for slash and gut. The boss likes his battles,
the unrepentant wallop of big guns,

a great lover of art, culture, and etiquette:
a connoisseur of all things pea soup.

Scaling the Great Wall of Joy

Another bumpy ride out to the Great Wall in a rattling pot-pan claptrap
assembled from recycled leftovers, siphoned halfway across the world.

This time you plan to walk eight kilometers along its peaks and troughs,
all the way to where brick starts to crumble, turns back to dense mud.

You've brought along your Austrian hiking boots, the ones that lace halfway
up your calves, a Nordic stick, and you're wearing a T-shirt that reads:

I've scaled Mount Everest, K2 and the Matterhorn.
Now I'm going straight for the Moon.

I dabble, sip tea in a small, flea-infested restaurant fifty strides away
from where buses collide in gray and white and blue, nibble roasted

pumpkin seeds, smoke half a pack of Five Stars and glare at a crowd:
mostly weekend honeymooners, Japanese legions with fluttering

triangular green flags that look like G-strings on sticks, and yellow peaked caps
that read: *Suzuki Cheese Tourist Agency. Always willing to please.*

There are Germans here too, hoping to find a bockwurst with mustard,
something meaty, just as they do along Costa Dorada most summers.

They're miffed, reduced to dribbling, then flinging, twirling chopsticks
like batons—peanuts, flecks of tofu, and rice fly too—and guzzling beer

that's kept alive with formaldehyde, rumbling, not quite arm in arm,
but I can feel an oompah-pah coming on, long before they breach the steps.

They're hoping to catch a glimpse of an emperor, a court eunuch or two,
after the marching band and the fireworks and a stately tea-pouring.

Three hours later and you're back, sporting a pink hue, no sun hat,
and a big purple gash straight across your moon-bound heart.

You're limping, like someone's bent or broken your spring.
Your T-shirt now reads:

I've scaled (blotch) and (blotch)
Now I'm going straight (blotch)

Snap-turtling at the waitress, you order yourself a long draft,
hoping for it chilled in a frosty mug, but it comes out warm and

thick as glue. I don't dare ask where you got the purple, but finally,
you tell me: Taiwan baby, mother's arms, taking photo, wrong time,

slushy nearly went straight in my face. I stifle a chuckle, but can't hold
back and you—you soon start to snigger too.

Dharma and the Goose

Lhasa, Tibet, 1999

In a room filled with battered prayer wheels, a nun reclines
on a beach chair, mumbles verses, liberating herself

through the intermediate, stepping closer to the final end
breath by breath.

We spin, watch them rattle and rasp, then stumble

upon a monastery tucked behind a wall. We stride right in
as if we thought we owned the place, like Mao.

Monks pay little heed, do laundry,
pat stray dogs,
           jostle and whip around
                a single deflated football.

Behind a heap of compost, over an archway, a pair of yak horns
eyes us down.

Inside, three monks print, fingering ink,
paper crawls in fluttering stanzas
                  like swimming
in the Tibetan Book of the Dead.

In a corner, an abbot, a white goose limp in his lap,
puffs directions,
        points,
            chatters,

strokes the goose, looks up, grumbles.

So where, you say, running fingers through your hair,
Where, my dear gentlemen, might a lady find a toilet?

Abbot stands,
           goose takes to air,
                circles, lands,
                      abbot claps hands:

You're nearly there. A nudge of the head, a beat of wings:

Behind the staircase.

        Over the bucket of tea.

            Under the mandala.
Stop.

     That's it.   *A little to the right.*

Watch the goose.

      It's where she lays her eggs.

           Mind your head.
Straight ahead.

May the Buddha bless you

      —and please, please flush before you go!

The General's Little Panda Paws

*In the parking lot of the Shanghai Waigaoqiao Customs
and Excise Building, Shanghai, 2000*

The General doesn't like to be kept waiting.
He'll be washing his hands a dozen times,
        scrubbing under his fingernails,
soaping his palms limber and white

        as he always does before every meal;
then he'll just sit there, legs crossed,
        smoking, puffing on his hot tea until it cools.
He won't drink it until you arrive;

        he'll just play with the leaves, watching
them fall and rise, until they sink
        to the bottom, fluttering there like seaweed.
Only then, he says, is it ready to sip,

when water and tea have become one.
        He's gone to a huge amount of trouble tonight,
flown in wood pigeons and birds' nest soup from Sichuan.
        You know how they harvest those nests?

Dangling on thin ropes on cliff sides at the crack of dawn.
        The General abhors eating alone.
We should give him a ring, only his assistant will never answer.
        She's stupid as they come.

You know why he hired her?
        It was her tiny feet. *Little Panda Paws* he calls her.
He told me once, he likes to watch her padding
        barefoot across the wooden floor of his office with hot tea.

It makes him think he's back three hundred years
              and she, his Spring Blossom who could never run away
even if she tried. Sometimes he takes her
              right there on his desk, wearing his medals, her apricot arse

plunked on top of all the papers like a perfect paperweight.
              He especially likes to do it on bank statements,
insurance policies, and shipping contracts,
              anything a little heavyweight.

Says, it helps him to lighten the burden.
              Hurry yourself, hurry yourself up.
You know full well he doesn't like to eat alone,
              and we can't let the General's tea get stone cold.

Kowtow

Hong Kong, 1951

As once Grandpa had said:
the seeds of power never fall
far from the flower.

He keeps repeating this
every night before death,
and on that last leg,

floating into Whampoa Harbor
in the eddies of oil and
war-bloated corpses,

the bump and groan,
the hiss of gastric acids—
and all those blind miles

of saltwater on his back
the sun's sting
and the gulls yelping

Cor! Cor! overhead
leading the sharks
straight to fishbait—

it's pure miracle
he makes it,
he kisses the sands

of Tai Mo Shan,
even eats a handful.
Freedom, he thinks,

tastes bittersweet,
and soon the fertile land
fills him,

crawls deep
under the skin,
and he digs his feet in.

Our Father Who Art in People's Square

Eat anything that has its back to the sky.
If you don't eat them, they will fly away.

—*Old Chinese Proverb*

Deft

The ornate,
the gilded
in Sun's corona,

the weather-washed
in light's retina,
figures

in the instant
of recognition,
a volition

of the volatile
looking for
fingertip, the

falter
of the touch
or the touched.

The Mystical Art of Accounting

When you have to deal with a beast you have to treat him as a beast…
—*Harry S. Truman*

It's all about volume,
capacity per square meter / foot
(whether metric or imperial floats your proverbial boat);
although, there are others
                    (a whole slew of choices, in fact):
the Tokyo *Tsubo* for instance; sounds like soy-infused Wasabi sauce;
the Seoul *Pyeong*: true measure of an average ninth century
        Korean male—
arms and legs fully splayed, face down prostrating, flailed by the brunt
of a Mongolian warlord's cat 'o nine tails, an ideal size for a room,
I am told; or perhaps face up, making perfect circles
under cherry blossoms in the snow, stargazing,
defining the rules of space and numbers.

                    Imperial Peking had,
and Social Democratic Communist Beijing
still has the *Mu*, which possibly derives it's name
from the exhausted groan of the water buffalo—
a measure for judging the extent of rice paddies before harvest.
Everything is weighted, ruled, cubed, boxed, angled, triangled—
lucky we came up with these handy things, numbers.

Now we can finally count the stars in the sky—
6000 with the naked eye—and we know useful things
like the distance from the equator to the moon
represents sixty-nine times the girth of a full grown earth.

                    Funny that, the number 69—
normally I think of being twenty one again,
in the back of my *Unbeatable Bonk Bug* with Maria-Rosa,
Hispanic-American goddess, gently calculating
trigonometric angles, postulating X/Y positions.

Without numbers we wouldn't know our up from down,
we wouldn't even know there are more than two of anything at all—
just be walking on straight lines in flat spaces, like Pacman,
we wouldn't know an arse from an elbow, really.
Yet, these are mostly distances—things men have conquered,
numbers have far reaching consequences:

Analysts know how much *Namibia* is worth on paper,
in *Dollars, Euros, Rupees;* its equivalent in derivatives;
and in conjunction with funded institutions of science,
how much bacteria and moss can contribute
to the global economic balance sheet—
it has all been tallied out, audited down
to the last decimal point, then stamped,
duly notarized and sealed in hot wax for posterity.

There is surely a secret book,
hidden in the darkest catacombs of the Vatican
where all calculations are indexed for future evidence;
or perhaps it is hermetically locked
in the sprawling prairies of Middle-America,
guarded by the Federal Agency in charge of numbers.

I mean, why else would they call it Area 51,
giving it not one, but two prime numbers?
And, by the way: 69 and 51 add up to 120,
which is a recurring number in the Mayan calendar,
and shall someday well fulfill an ancient prophesy
unlocking the last secrets of the Universe.

Yes, we have developed all sorts of uses for numbers;
we know how many atoms are required in an atom bomb,
but more importantly how much it costs,
(2 billion dollars for Harry Truman in 1945, 20 billion dollars today);
there must be reasons, of course, why God gave us five fingers on each hand—
he wanted us, it seems, to count on them. One by one by one.

Atomkraft 1967

Zhong Guo means the middle country;
the middle way, the path to liberation.

Coal thieves on scooters
dig from the middle of the earth,
separate the temporal from the permanent,
burn fires that melt iron ore
and draw curtains over the skies.

The old man wished for the atom bomb,
but Stalin wouldn't give it to him.

In 1967, he got it.

He dredged fish from lifeless rivers,
fed souls with limp clothes
and hungry eyes.

As we were told, in our Village Cooperatives
and People's Communes,
real miracles could happen.

In 1970, he launched satellites
straight into heaven,
to give us an eye
on the world.

I've been told you can't split the atom
any way but down the middle.

Another Satisfied Customer

We phoned. Quite analytically we
dissected its molecular structure.

And how it made Grandma Liu
all woozy when she woke.

It conflicted with her porridge,
made her bridge chatter, even if

her gums were doing most
of the work. And you know what

they said? They said it had something
to do with politics. The etiquette of

the matter. Yes, it struck a chord
in the hearts of us all. They were

uncomfortable to say the least.
But what could they do? It was

only a job, after all. You couldn't
blame them for something that wasn't

of their own making. Just a soldier
they said, taking orders from the

head office. Would you believe it?
We'd a right mind to write to

our local Party secretary. But then,
we decided against it and drew

Grandma Liu's morning bath with
that oil that makes her smell of roses.

Abduction

Lin Hao Liu, Zhe Xi Agricultural Commune, Guangxi Province, 2001

My wife was stolen right under my nose, just like the eggs that red fox
    pilfers from my prize chickens—only he leaves a yolky trail.

They say she was sold to a Mongolian who fells trees with his bare hands
    and speaks Russian without the trace of an accent.

She's pregnant with his child once again and because he's a minority,
    he's allowed to have ten.

My daughter hired an undercover sleuth and we travelled far north
    to Hohhot to talk sense with the local police.

They said nothing could be done: *Your child is your own and all grown
up, and the woman you used to call your wife has other obligations.*

I knew it was a question of hard cash, and while I was sitting there
    in the boarding house with my daughter and the sleuth,

the secret police came to arrest me. They said if I didn't sign the
    divorce papers, they would see me in chains.

I'm only a simple farmer. I grow watermelons. I've nothing much to offer
    but a life of hard work and boiling sun.

Under an Auspicious Eye, the Monkey King, Karl Marx, Charles Darwin and Mao Zedong Do Breakfast at the Four Seasons

—for Arthur Waley

Hey, ho! says the Monkey King tucking
into rashers of bacon entirely forgetting
that his dear friend Piggy (whom
he journeyed to the West with) was entirely pig.

Welcome Comrades! says Mao, digging
into scrambled eggs; and, to the disgust of all,
leaves his cigarette smoldering and rests his oily chopsticks
on the tablecloth like a real country bumpkin.

Years in caves will do that, mutters Karl who abstains
from solids, and sips ladylike on his coffee, which by the way
he prefers cool as he says it burns his sensitive lips
(without which, he might not talk like a reformer).

Charles, in his absent fashion,
orders himself an entire grilled fish which Mao says
has been plucked straight from the Yangtze and fattened
on all manner of swarming insects, dragonflies mainly.

The Monkey King sniggers, and having wiped his plate clean,
somersaults over to the buffet for seconds. Karl glances
at Mao and Charles and says perhaps
they should not have invited the uncouth ape.

Mao goes quite white and reminds the other two
that the Monkey King was born from a solid stone egg. And, in case
they had forgotten, says: *Stone is the bedrock of a nation.*
Charles, sucking the eyes from his fish, says:

Yes, Mao. You're quite right. It entirely slipped our minds.

And somewhere in the lobby tucked behind
his tabloid, and a headline that reads,

Wisdom Comes in Many Guises!

the Buddha is sipping a gin and tonic, and chuckling.

Even Keel

Chairman Mao taught us:
Conquer nature to free yourself from it.

and he swam the Yellow River
with a cigarette smoking in one hand.

When I returned from university
all we got were snapshots of dead fish and rusty cans,

and a man with a striped Italian tie said:
The pillars of the economy are powerful taxpayers.

We listened, only the forest didn't
as grassland turned to desert and
desert turned to moonland.

But we were told not to fret, for the Man will build
a new socialist countryside for us all.

He will make new rivers
to balance out God's unfairness.

Rabbit

Shanghai People's Park, Sunday Morning, 2007

'Snap, snap it went,
quick as kindling.

A teddy bear
without the stuffing.

And the little girl
cried and cried.

Had her tears
been rain, I'm sure

it would have
come alive—all Frankenstein.

Yet even when
the ear came tearing off

and blood was spewing
everywhere

my Great Dane was barking
the little girl deaf.

She hugged it to her
white dress until she was

all red, tattered
and barely alive.

I gave the man two bills.
He nodded and we left it at that.'

Pocketful of Crickets

A Weekend Jaunt into Backcountry

Jiangxu, Jiangsu Province 2003

Every fine morning you can see these ancient playboy merchants trudging to their favorite corners carrying their precious cargo with them. There they assemble their stock, carefully separating rusty screws from crooked nails, and there they sit all day in the sun.

—*Carl Crow, 400 Million Customers, Harper & Brothers, New York, 1937*

1. Bazaar

Lunar Festival weasels round, sniffing at the open heart of a trash-strewn market.

We gawk at ear-cleaners plunge swizzle sticks, & wonder what the hell they do with all that wax.

Here are veritable bargains: scraps of underpants & neon feather-dusters, dusty kids gnashing purple sugarcane, rubbing hands pink in the brisk morning, & plastics:

compressed soap dishes, ravioli-makers, Chanel makeup cases for powder puffs.

We scrutinize piles, rows displayed like the first catch of the day, forced to endure Canto-pop blaring from a foghorn at decibels that make it spit, crack & fuzz & make our heads throb; a distraction is hoping to find some forgotten gem—

yet everything is something we've seen before: Che Guevara T-shirts, Gucci bags with the 'C's backwards, New York Dodgers' caps, Hello Kitty pencils, footballs signed by David Beckham lined up like sugar-frosted wedding cakes.

2. Boom

One old bloke, a moth-eaten woolly cap (emblazoned with a Shell logo) tugged down over his ears is flogging yams smoking over a sawn-off oil barrel; his roadside companion, wet flannel draped over her head, is having her teeth bored by a man pumping his feet like he's playing the pipe organ. The drill bit looks like it fell off some deep sea oil rig, but she leans back uncomplaining to take deep steel & echoes hollow gurgles.

We've come all the way to witness miracles in the backcountry as it was before the boom; yet all that holds firm are the aged, the children & the second-quality rejects.

Mums & Dads normally stockpiling in factories are now migrating back to their place of birth, shoaling in from Shanghai, Beijing, Qingdao & further south, the vast assembly lines of Fuzhou & Xiamen, Guangdong & Datong, trawling gifts galore in overflowing suitcases:

things you can't find back hometown: soft-shell crab & Harbin fish roe & Australian Beef & Marlboro & coffee from a can—Blue Mountain imported all the way from Jamaica (but hand-roasted in Yunnan).

3. Council

Bing hasn't been back since 1998. At the train station Ba Ba looks shriveled; with three long whiskers he's an ancient catfish & his threadbare Mao suit wobbles.

Bing is no chip off the old block, rather a compact version of his bedridden mother who raises herself to prepare her famous egg-fried rice with tomatoes, coughing in hacking fits.

Glad we brought that bottle of Jack—it disinfects, pulverizes tapeworm—at least that's what Jerry an American backpacker told me on the train ride while sipping Longjin tea.

> *We've got much in store*, says Bing.
> *Meetings with the mayor, the village council.*
>
> *The Governor is taking us out for dinner.*
> *Better put on a tie.*

4. Governor

The Governor's office is baked in terracotta, no concrete floor & the walls are whitewashed in grizzled streaks. His assistant pours hot green cha in chipped cups that look like they've been used for digging in the garden.

I sip one cautious swig for face then leave the rest festering cold.

> *Not exactly what I would think of as a*
> *governor's office,* you say. *Needs a*
> *decent lick of paint for a start.*

> Bing says: *No, no. You don't understand.*
> *It's got to look poor. If he had a nice office*
> *the others would rumble & complain.*

Motto tacked behind the desk reads:

Keep it simple, don't tempt fate

Masquerading his pot belly behind a fluffy cashmere sweater, the Governor steps out of the newest Mercedes with knobs & buttons (which he says his kids can't get enough of).

Three gold teeth sparkle in the falling haze of a pink sun, & he smokes like Marlene Dietrich, chattering away in operatic sing-song. In between bursts, he punctuates the recycled air with light, garlic-infused burps.

It seems he's already eaten once tonight, perhaps twice—a fleck of dumpling shimmers on his collar.

5. Banquet

Tucked deep in back upper stories buck-teethed serving girls escort us to courtly chambers. Here lords & ladies gather to impress visiting dignitaries.

Bing whispers:

> *Perhaps they'll give me a loan—better drink a lot.*

& the Mao Tai—at over 60 proof & clear as clean water—flows.

The Governor, three provincial mayors, four city council members & two local business leaders raise glasses:

> *Ganbei!*

& down the hatch it goes—like sulfuric acid—seems to hiss & whine as it nudges crick by crick, cleaning my esophagus free.

Bing pinches me under the table:

> *Tell them how much you adore their city.*

I muster complimentary puffs and praises: views & vistas, impressive artifices, world's oldest civilization, great vibe of new commerce.

> *Great to be with you,* I bellow. *Hang Hao Che!*

> *Pieces of heaven.*

> & then: *Ganbei!* Again.

6. Fish-Eyed

The food arrives.

It's enough to feed Mao's armies on the Long March, smothered in
sauces, leaking essential oils, there's hardly a food group ignored:
A dish of deep-fried scorpions skirts the inner sanctum; the Governor
has three fingers on the Lazy Susan, it's almost as if he's scratching hip
hop beats:

dance of the twiddling fingers & *Hey Presto!*

Here are the mixed crickets & black beetles,

Whoops! here come the toads & maggots.

     Glorious, splutters Bing,

plowing in with sticks, bits of fat flying. A wing sticks out of his mouth
like an origami swan, but it's polished off with another swig of lip-
glistening Mao Tai.

The Governor sucks his tea like he's switched on his vacuum-cleaner:
Rummph! farts, belches, picks up his own sticks, & click-click prods
the vermin—almost as if to double-check if anything here is alive.

You stare at me fish-eyed.

I pick one cherry off the crispy pile, it's about as big as my thumb &
flash-fried in grimace.

     Adore these, says Bing dredging the bowl.

Bits of legs, antennae & skeletons pile his plate.

     When I was a kid, I used to climb the
     trees near my house. I'd perch on a branch for hours

then catch them with my very own fingers.
They're best when they're fresh.

You whisper,

      …& chirping

.

I close my eyes, crunch & gulp: no taste whatever: It oozes & crackles
in its shell.

7. *Fortitude in Motion*

I spend all night on the toilet between sips of *Jack*. You can't stop yourself chuckling:

Cricket diarrhea!

Next morning we elbow through the dumpling sellers, hot milk & yoghurt carts, thousands crouch spitting melon pips, fish bones. Some still doze on red & blue striped ten-liter shopping bags, soldiers chain-smoke Red Pagoda cigarettes.

We make it inside. Bing's booked us first class—he looks like he hasn't caught a minute of shuteye.

He's beaming though.

> *It's good you can drink. Europeans are strong.*
> *The Governor's going to have a word*
> *with his friend at the Bank of China.*
> *Now I can finally start my factory.*

He unravels a little jiffy bag from his pocket, pops a fried cricket in his mouth.

> *Breakfast,* he mumbles, crunching—

Still Life with Cherry Blossoms and Concubine Playing the Pipa

I'll never forget you, least of all in my mind

    and when I'm lucky, you'll materialize in a dream or two,

plucked from a meticulous still life, flourishing like spring

    from your hair and lips, the wistful concubine beside her emperor,

and a yellow butterfly perched gently on the end of your pipa,

    the metaphor, an insight into your cosmic joke,

subservience concocted in a wistful image

    of a woman and an insect and a transcendental note.

Sea Slug

Qingdao Most Unusual and Assorted Dishes Restaurant,
Shandong, August 1997

doing nothing
the sea slug lives
a million years
—Shiki Namako

I earned my home with sweat
typing fifty words a minute on six fingers.

A little blood never hurt anyone,
but I always feared the prick of the needle.

I've also a mighty fear
of the sea slug.

He stares you down from the plate
with a hundred shifty needlepoint eyes.

Even when he's bone-dead,
you swear he's still alive.

Baby One

Chengdu People's Hospital, Sino-American Joint Venture Ward,
Szechuan, 2001

Delicate as skinning a snake,
they eased her out with a knife.
One long scar remains from my heart
just above my pelvic bone.
They say she came out folded.
Stamped. Like she was ready to be
posted to some distant corner,
bent right over like a carnival acrobat.

You know they train those children
to fit into jam jars when they're young.
I said: *Doctor, was it something I ate?*
He said: *Wouldn't want you to take the blame*
for all those things they put in your meat.
That evening my husband drove me home
quietly in his new Mercedes.
He'd piled cushions all around
and didn't breathe a word.

Next morning over breakfast he said:

My baby was very nearly born, yesterday.

The State-Owned Entity is Like
an Extended Family

Better get your wife to buy you as pot of strong-scented flowers.
You see, Xu only takes a wash once a week at a public bath.

His house doesn't have a toilet, only an outhouse
down a mud path, over planks.
                    Regular as clockwork is Xu.

He's been with us twenty years; here, you have a job for life:
the company is good to her staff.

                    Note all the pens on your desk,
and a note pad, fresh from the printers with a brand new logo
designed by yours truly.

                    Can you believe? It came to me while I was
on the bus home one eve.
This job inspires true creativity.
All young men's dreams can be fulfilled here, in true socialist fashion.

There's one computer, it's in room three-o-five, down the hall.

I check every fax personally, so make every word count; and English,
everything in the Queen's English. No dashes, no run-on sentences:
we don't want dilly-dalliers here.

Course, you can take the simple approach, like Xu:

The path of least resistance is the true path of righteousness.

One-upmanship is something we frown upon, it's like desire.
it brews fetid, spreads dissent. The will of the people, brotherhood,
sisterhood. We believe in true equality.

You are quite familiar with The Book, I take it? We read together at five.

And, don't be afraid to criticize, you know, deviant behavior,
lustful eyes in the canteen, old poetry, capitalist philosophy;
anything untold.
        Keep an eye out.

You know there's always truth in a rumor.
That's what the notepad is for. Do well, and you and your wife
shall have everything required for an ideal life. Expecting is she?

You'll like it here, you'll see.

The Interrogatory

Failure to meet tight deadlines—
a nagging, or perhaps an itch to fight back
against the morass, your tender
gardening pleasures, the Zen
of green thumb, the nurturing of integers
where a plus didn't mean more than this
and a negative was just another tax haven
until—as had frequently been divined,
cross-legged in rapt meditation, staring
in to the Mists of Lake Hangzhou
a hesitation arrived, something
did not multiply. Lucky for you
the world was no solid ball, but a spongy
mass that gave way and bounced back.

Six Stages of Moral Growth
in a United Motherland

—

One voice one mind
Outside looking in
Inside looking out
One Party one Justice
Grassroots working up
Big smile looking down

二

The only way
to find the middle path
is to dilute the unique.
Homogenize and oppose
any form of independence. [1]

三

If you are a Party member
you can only have one belief:
The belief in the Motherland,
in the organized state of mind,
is the only religious party of the State.
The party is like the mother.
She has nurtured
all the younger generation.

---

[1] *Separatist activities?*
We classify these as terrorist.
If anyone uses religion to effect national security,
we'll crack down on them in accordance with the law.
Religion must be strictly controlled. It's only permitted
in the form of a hobby like stamp collecting.

四

The struggle for the cause
is the goal of all progressive
healthy young people.
To achieve one united Motherland is
a long process that can
be divided in six even stages.

五

This is how we will become
a prosperous society.
The Party is Mother-Creator
for the conditions for prosperity
and perceives the interests
of all the people.

六

When in doubt, remember:
the Good Minister says:
The laboring masses
must ride the tide
of material civilization
and build success
on the battlefield
of economic construction.

Please contact your local Propaganda Department to obtain
a high quality printed, perfect-bound handy pocketbook
signed by your Chairman, free of charge.

Sweater

Chaozhou Open Air Textile and Leather Goods Market, 2001

—for Leslie T. Chang

All I want is a sweater,
made to fit, not too tight—

see, it shouldn't pinch my arms,
be too loose around the neck,

and make sure you stitch
the details well, last one

fell apart when I was washing it
in the bath, the dye flowed out

and my hands were
stained like beetroot.

I know your prices are keen,
still, it's nice to wear the thing

more than once. You're shaking
your head. You can't control

the quality of the thread, and
the dye, the dye you bought

from a reputable supplier.
All I want is a sweater,

one that damn well fits.

Letter to My Beloved Husband
in a Beijing Prison

Beijing, November 27, 2007

Dearest Husband,

Loyal Communist Party Under-Secretary,
Manager of the award-winning branch
of the Wu Xu People's Agricultural Bank:

You count bills fingertip to tongue—
leafed like precious lotus petals, bundle them
in tight pink bricks for those who toe the line
with sturdy iron wheelbarrows.

One evening you arrive late and dinner sits hard:
a heap of fish eyes beading you down quite ashen grey.

Usually you've a bear's appetite, slurping, sucking, chomping
in breaths of spiced delight, but now you burn vacantly,
nursing Grandpa Liu's homemade rice wine.

Normally I use it for cleaning windows.

What is it, Heart of Hearts? I ask, as you rest chin to palm
and sigh frostlike, as if across January winds.

Your tireless boss, our faithful Communist Party Adjudicator
has rubber-stamped a construction loan, you say?
to a company without a solitary spade, only loose fingers
in Virgin Islands swishing in the swell of a piss-warm Sargasso sea?

The old fart tried to cut you in, 'Purse your lips, Boy,' he coughed;
Then grinned with five-percent top-skimmed:

Oh, that lizard has hands like flypaper.

I told you his father, a warlord, was coddled at knifepoint
by Big Ears Du. I, loyal wife, say: Eat! Heart of Hearts, for soon
you must alight and report this with due diligence to those who toll
the great brass bell near the Temple of Heaven.

You leave as pink dawn spikes morning dew and garlic shrimp
rattles in snap-lock on the serpent sleeper train, swerving
all the way north.

I call you in sick, say you're feverish, shivering blue.
But on my line, Heart of Hearts you don't ring.
My female intuition bubbles and brews.

Little Xi and I follow, with knapsacks; she in pigtails;
I, clipped close to match my scowl. We rattle three nights
            with fruit bats
chirping in our chests and tigers growling in our heads.

But when we arrive they cuff us and chain us
in a single cell overlooking proud Longevity Hill with the pagoda
and the dapple of Kunming Lake.

We watch swans swimming behind bars.

Little Xi is eight years old.

After three months, we are let loose to roam
the charcoal-walled Hutongs.

We doze in wet corridors, beneath the wilting stalks
of other people's bamboo where monstrous black rats ignore us.

We, without a home and two left feet.

150

Little Xi can no longer stand, so I carry
her like a rice sack on my back.
Even as you,
Heart of Hearts, still smolder inside your walls,
I gather rubbish behind hospitals: syringes, cotton wads
and single purple pills
for medical factories in the backcountry.

We pray they will release you, beloved,
when they have finished white-washing the world

in those magnificent Olympic games.

Your loving wife, patiently.

Speaking in Tongues

Alluvial soils. Layers sifted
upon the breach of olden times.
Evidence of the civilized civilizing.

Any grand man buried with his pride,
his ego placed fittingly in his mouth like jade
that he should not swallow his own tongue.

And should a man outlive his wife
may she have been his queen alive
that in his old age he might recall

the wonders she once gifted him.
In all that is life he should subside
to rediscover his name on her tongue.

And in lesser times, ages now passed
remembered as the glory days of blood and promises,
that the widow and widower are

a reflection of each other,
the mirror of all that has transpired
and set upon this earth to taste her spices.

Two of a Pair, Four of a Kind

Lin Yu Yu Tea & Cake Shop, Yangzhou, Jiangsu Province, 1990

Xiu Er breaks the deck.

Hao Ban: Old proverb says:
When the big tree falls,
all the monkeys run away.

        Hua Guo Feng's four monkeys
were the Chairman's eyes, ears, lips
and the hands that smothered them.

Xiu Er: Even when the old boy slept in bed
his shadow loomed over the middle kingdom
and monkeys rattled in his ribs.

Hao Ban: But when he died, the forest laid bare,
and the great tree at its center started to rot.

Xiu Er: The monkeys plucked him bare. No fruit.

Hao Ban lights a *Zhongnanhai* cigarette. Shuffles.

Hao Ban: It'd be a pity not to have any fruit anymore.
I need my watermelons when it's hot outside.

Xiu Er: Melons don't grow on trees—least not here in the city,
but one hundred flowers bloom on the skyline.

Hao Ban: My uncle always used to say:
Flowers are pretty, but they cannot fly.

Xiu Er: Lin Biao flew though didn't he?

Xiu Er deals.

Hao Ban: He crashed on his way to Mister Stalin.

Xiu Er: Old proverb says:
             A bird can't land
             if there's no branch to perch on.

Hao Ban folds.

V

The Buddha's Last Firecrackers

Even if I am crushed into powder,
I will embrace you with the ashes

—Liu Xiaobo, Chinese poet & political prisoner

Winter Falls in Shanghai

The eternal moan of taxis
grumbling of distances still to shuttle,
through thin walls
sleep comes slow
and single-paned windows
eye the sweep of smoggy night
and the lost creep into your bed,
all the way under your skin.

I hug you tighter here
than anywhere else in the world.

It's the only way I sleep at night.

And in the morning
where are the singing birds?

No Birds

Early Shanghai mornings, window unzipped,
Hard tinny noises titter & trill & honk,
Shatter & ripple, yet, nowhere do sea birds skim:

No trash-pan kittiwakes, no lonesome terns fading
In mussel-caught pinpricks of sky dust,
Not a single sandpiper clowning carnival eights.

The wind smells burnt, sulfur-singed hot,
Charcoaled, as if he has been lying about everything,
Entirely unattended on the smoke-oil steel of wok.

Some Tarzan cleans the dizzy horizon with dirty rags,
Arcs pendulous on a single thread of corded hope.
Minutes later, memory wiped, window squeezed tight.

Inside, pigeons squirt bombs from the ceiling,
Grebes nest in my hair, a peacock struts the kitchen pecking crumbs
& the fattest phoenix of them all sits right here in the bath,

Preening, plashing away all that murky ash and dust.

Hear it? She's singing, as if in heaven.

Indefinite Measures

Listen.

Summer has arrived.

Can you not hear the orioles

singing in the willows?

The warmth of South rises,

and with that swell, you,

you unravel, shedding

your thinnest skins.

K.Y.

at the Mandarin Oriental Hotel, Hong Kong, 1989

Kwok Ying thinks people of a certain kind
will find it easier to remember him. He's right.

But as if his name were so hard to inflect—
plenty of other things come to mind.

Memory works in flashbacks,
scraps of trailers, web-bytes, top-ten charts, ding-a-ling.

Still, he's called me here for a reason,
not just to watch him plow through a 15-oz. steak,

French fries, Brussels sprouts all doused in Béarnaise,
slurping and sucking like he's got to get it all in before it's too late.

I sit back, watching it all unfold:
genius at the dinner plate.

Twenty minutes in, chewing for his life,
he rustles it out of his jacket pocket:

typewritten on carbon paper.
Here. For you. Careful. He says.

Inside there's a number with five zeros.
An ooze of sauce drips onto his sleeve.

We have coffee. He has a crêpe suzette, flambéed with cognac.
At the end he reaches for the bill, says: *So? We have deal?*

Crushed Dragon Bones

Tiger Claw Apothecary, Shanghai, 1999

Quan leads me through an array of popping scents,
this lingering whiff of Bombay spice bazaar,

medicine healing scars, prehensile fungi, blooming
rhino horn, white deer antler, mandible of stag beetle,

snapping tail of scorpion, turtle snout, all crushed to steep
in clear hot liquids bubbling right into the very center

of the maze where a woman in a nightdress waits patiently.
Here he goes whispering in the corner.

Lady behind the counter turns flushed-cheek red,
titters under her breath, holds her hand to cover her teeth.

Eyes him apprehensively. Eyebrows arch-raised,
coughs in syncopated answer. Fiddles with her stethoscope.

Another woman looks me up and down: *Hey you, big nose?*
Want me check your pulse? I sit down across the counter.

She applies the leather-puffing contraption to my left bicep.
Pumps until I feel my left side is ready to explode.

Aha, take this. She fiddles a powder, rattling grains from
that drawer, granules from another. All marked in red.

Grinds the mixture in mortar humming some old love tune.
Flips the dust into a paper bag. Hand palm out:

Fifty Yuan. Releases the catch and *Ssssss* spins down.
Quan's smiling ear to ear and we're out the door

through the hedgerows and into haze of open space.
Quan rumbles something about *bones old bones.*

Crushed dragon bones for the little man inside.
No problem like you, he says. *This will keep me going all night.*

Violin Wang and the Swan

(1)

Above the gulag, where wolves snarl hidden in the shadows of a blue forest, Alfred plans to purchase pink PP-5 pellets, wrap them in Dutch heraldry—three lions roaring *je maintiendrai*—then foist them upon the unarmed through heresy. For the job, he sequesters 2 former Soviet spies, a Swiss businessman down on his luck & a Cantonese geezer named Violin Wong who rubs elbows with Shanghai Customs & Excise.

In Tomsk, asphalt conjoins gravel, gravel becomes mud, mud becomes pond & frog, then potholes back to asphalt again. Nothing cruises in straight lines; it has the feel of a natural order of things. & the man from Zurich in the Burberry raincoat can't hold down his grub even after successive infusions of Siberian snakebite. He blurts & ruffles & flushes & flushes, wriggling on his coattails like a peacock trying to lay three golden eggs in a thorny nest.

& the two Soviet spies don't reappear on the 2nd day.

On the 3rd, Albert gets a ring from a woman with a sandpaper voice whom he thinks wears a bright red scarf bundling her head & who raps the table with twiddling spider-fingers: *Alles kaput!* she says.

(2)

Albert witnesses the entrails of crumbling homes decorated in posters of Rambo & country-French faux, where lettuce is a rare commodity & trades for sticks of dynamite, & a bear of a Cossack named Nikolae strums balalaika with three missing fingers. On the 4th, Georgyii Kalashnikov, grandson of the inventor of the AK-47 & General Manager of workshop no. 7 proves he has just as much spunk & signs a Letter of Intent on tiptoe with a 4-bottle Stolichnaya glow. Violin trembles & the burning in his larynx cajoles so he take on the quiver of a cello.

Among the firs in Georgyii's wooded sauna, the red-welt smear of Siberian slapping hands becomes a Neolithic cave painting on Violin's bony back. Standing there towel to waist, stars glowing neon overhead like Wanchai brothels & a wolf snorting behind a barbed wire fence, Georgyii raises a final toast.

Blessings to the Crown Prince of Orange!
Long Live Chairman Mao!

(3)

Back at the hotel, before Albert sleeps there's a rap at the door. It's Violin in his Y-fronts cradling a black swan, a heavenly creature that purrs like a Siamese cat. A gift, he says, from the man with the gun. Would you just look at those eyes, he says, snuggling down into Albert's bed.

& on the 5th, the morning of the flight, Albert raises his head from vodka-dead & finds a few black feathers, a gray speckled egg nestled on the pillow & a note that reads:

Help me, Dutchman. I've fallen wildly in love.

Pig

Hai Nan Island, 1997

You crucified a pig
    on the beach
        & doused it
            with salty ocean.
                Once a fisher of fish,
            your hook a rusty nail
        bent by iron hands.
    In the old days,
an English girl
    in a striped bikini
        adored the way
            you hair played
                like waves and
            your laugh lines
        that plumbed deep.
    You savored her
for three nights,
    then purred as
        she stroked you
            to sleep.
                That, you said,
            was the real sum
        of your rip-roaring
    adventures.
And when the hog
    was blistered
        and the skin slipping off,
            like a layer
                of melting ice,
            dripping & spitting,
        you ate it, tearing
      piece by succulent piece
until, warmed-through,

you murmured
              like big cats.
                    When you awoke
                          the sun was coming
                    alive again:
              a bloom of stinking
        red algae frothing
on the shore.
        And behind,
              the skull of a pig
                    stared at an invisible
                          curvature of earth.

Mole

That thing under Mao's lip?
You call it a wart,
she calls it a beauty mark.

The principal architect of a new China
had moles all over the place,
hair plucked with fine tweezers.

Mao spoke of guerrillas
as insurgent fish
in a sea of promise,

said that's how Sun Tzu
taught him to beat
the man who ran off to Taiwan.

Personally,
I think it has everything
to do with the mole.

Ling Guo Lu Whispers
(Building C4 Apartment F12-03)

Government Official Housing Estate, Chang'An District, Beijing, 1992

we'll slip past the guard post behind the bicycle shed
but watch those potted geraniums
                              imagine where the guards piss

when it's belting down like this the toilet's just too far
& old boys don't sprint
                              they have our heartfelt understanding

that's Peng Fu: he comes on late; don't worry, mostly he's asleep
when he isn't puffing
                              Double Happiness or counting girls

in bright pink lipstick flying by in yellow taxis, he can sleep anywhere
even standing at attention
                              fish-eyed

the Minister of Foreign Affairs lives over there in a barbed compound
beyond that rhododendron
                              hold your umbrella low

at a pinch we might just be delivering Fedex or Dominos, wave
at the guy who trims the hedges
                              hovering in the shadows

now you see how we really live in our own mundane normality
ready to do business with anyone, really
                              Africans, Eskimos, Caucasians, Gypsies

last week I sold three containers of padlocks to a cursing Arab
next I have two Jew guys from Brazil
                              can barely read their lips

lucky I have such an adaptable head, my father says one for numbers
duck: this wasn't made for people
                              over one-seventy

we all used to be six centimeters smaller, now even Grandma Ling
gets meat & fish & soy sauce & wine
                              four times a week

her bones are like Teflon & she plods to the market with her stroller
make sure you look down
                              Mrs Wang might size you up

when she peers through her peephole, she lounges in there all the day
waiting to see who passes on the stairs
                              & doesn't have a TV

gave it to the secret police for taking good care of her son
he's been shipped off to far-away Gansu
                              to be re-educated

in the way of the people–ah, here we are, we've reached the twelfth floor
don't be concerned about the bars
                              they keep the unwanted inside

like Luo Ban Hu who's had a tiff with the Premier, and this little girl
in a hat and woolly mittens is my wife, so sorry
                              she doesn't speak English

but look at that smile, why is she all bundled up, here, indoors
don't all pregnant women in the world do that
                              she won't take a bath for weeks

poor soul, you know a baby takes its mighty toll & wind carries the ghosts
of greedy ancestors, in the afterlife
                              they can't bear to be alone

here, have some peanuts, would you like nice a glass of warm Coca-Cola
it's all she drinks, good for the complexion
                              shall we head out

there's a great karaoke bar down the road, Russian girls, one Tom Collins
and you can have them for hours, and afterwards
                              to a 24-hour restaurant

where they serve chow dog, you must try the stir-fry with roasted
cashews & the sauce that burns hot in the throat

Admirable Kingdom

Hervé's Tintin cinched it—the illusion that on our one trip to Tibet—
we might catch a glimpse of the Abominable Snowman.

But I'll tell you:
I knew long before that this was not the missing link to our past.

Even on the highest peaks in crampons and sticks: nothing.
You suggested we might yet discover the unknown.

A lost scroll, perhaps? A manuscript would connect us
to the New World in undecipherable hieroglyphs.

Did I mention
the highlanders' shawls reminded me of the Andes?

Could it be, you said, that here was a displaced race of the Olmeca?
The ancestors of the Aztecs? Surely it was written in the stones.

I could see the need for some alternate history,
but in amongst the *stupas* and prayer flags, the yaks and butter tea

on Lake Nam-Tso where fish swim higher than most birds
and thousands circumnavigate rubbing elbows
        to the memory of Siddhartha,

there was only loneliness, dry wind upon the plains,
a certain kind of choking breathlessness.

In Gudje, lost kingdom of sand-hewn castles upon the rock of heavens,
the caretaker swept sand from sand,

feather-dusting the worn window-ledges and alcoves.
Anything to keep the desert from swallowing his heritage.

But even he—wind-bitten, grumpy old chap that he was—
had to smile at a photo of the Dalai Lama embracing the world.

Waiting in Line at the Petition Bureau

Petitioning is like drinking poison to quench a thirst.
— He Weifang

As long as we can live in peace, no light is ok.

What is a plea but a pain in an official's ass?

What do all these people lining up mean to you?

They mean someone hasn't done their job.

I've looked for answers most of my life.
Last time, I was bundled into a car by four men.

I asked them what did I do?

What did they say?

That I should be hard at work.

Petitioning is for Grandmas and Grandpas,
not for the greater good, they said,
then beat me silly.

The River, Once

once she went to quench
then she went to scrub

now she collects dead toads
grinds them with cornmeal to feed her sows

once she ploughed the land
toiled with her face deep in dark soil

her back burning in hot sun
now she works in the paper mill

making laminated labels for the city
sundays she takes a out boat

not to take in the view or dream
but to gather plastic bags

now she drinks from water bottles
carted here all the way from the city

label reads: pure filtered glacier water
and says it's drawn from a mountain

it reminds her of a spring
at the foot of a sleeping dragon

Fossil Record

Time told backward
until we are just about a thought,
cuckoos play wooden drums
to an audience of trees,
river weed claps & icy rivers only just born
have no idea of the salt-taste of sun's sweat,
fish have not yet begun
to drag, let alone walk
& little does anyone know of steel nets
that will peel back and expose everything.

Wrapped Up

Going home from school, Little Xu and Fatty Ma
found a paper box in the cornfield.

It was tied with cotton string
and inside the box was a dead baby.

They knew she must be an enemy of the people
because she had not died in the hospital.

They stoned the tiny body
and set their minds to rest.

When they got home it was Little Xu's birthday
and they had his favorite sweet bean buns for supper.

Barking Mad in the Gobi Desert

Father's a Taoist, Mother's a Kiwi, says the boy,
recommending the spiked omelet.
And how old are you, young lad?

> *Mother says gentleman never ask,*
> *besides I see you appreciate the sand.*

and then for a moment he becomes a man
as he stares over his unending dunes
where scraps of plastic snag on rock and twig—

and mangy dogs root in piles near the outhouse.
Surely he can't be more than ten years old.

> *And what of This World?* he asks
> *pointing out into the twilight sky.*

> *What do you make of it?*

Five minutes later his eggs are bleeding red pepper
and he returns with three nips of something
deconstructing in the back of his mind:

> *This is the Spike,* he says, *downing his glass.*
> *Mother tells me New Zealand oysters*
> *are the best in the world.*

and somewhere someone's fingering a *liuqin*.
A desert gypsy sings to sand and stars
and as if reading my mind, he says:

> *Here a good sleep is worth a million and*
> *a godly dream is something to cherish.*

and so I stumble downstairs to no electricity
to silent walls etched from nimble hands
blanked in a clouds of cloudy windows.

and suddenly it begins, that chorus of lost animals—
you'd think a whole world of dogs had descended
as the howls and the barks and the growls and the yelps

and the coughs and the barks of the rabid
serenade us into the sifting sands
of these godly dreams.

Sky-Swimming

Short escape of luminous days among fir trees and slopes
thick with crowberries along the spine of the Kunlun mountains

we sneak a shivering glance through the snow into the dreams'
shadow and the louvered darkness of cabin pressure

I think I'm about to sleep when you nudge me and point
through a crack in space between what we can and cannot see:

aircraft wing
        cumulous cloud
              and lightly
                        as if on the sea's skin
                                  something ancient
                                            sky-swimming

Tentacled dragon!

        barks the man beside me scrambling for his iPhone
but when he's finger-ready it has feathered

into a body
        of mist
                and haze
                        and sideways rain

How to Marry a Millionaire

While waiting her turn at the Recruitment Center
Su Ji reads a book called *Why Men Love Bitches*.
Her numbered ticket functions as a bookmark

when she goes to the toilet,
lifts her eyes for a scan of the competition—
or even better, susses out a self-made man.

Su Ji flaunts the book as if it were red-hot,
uses it as a paperback fan covering 'Why'
and 'Men' and 'Love' with her thumb.

She's not like those timid secretaries on the tube,
style-geeks who smother books in brown paper sheaths
encasing romance and thrillers like Mishima

shrouding S&M in metaphors, biding time
until rooftop hara-kiri. Su Ji's mother
always said: "If you can't marry

a boy from the village, have your sights set
high in the stratosphere. If you live too far away
to come home, at least you can fly in your money."

"I don't care if my husband-to-be has a head
like an over-cooked dumpling,
he needs to pamper me," says Su Ji.

In three grueling years she's gone
from assembly-line worker to office clerk.
Evenings with her bangs pinned in Swarovski barrettes

she swats flies and learns executive English.
She's taken crash courses on how to hold a fork and knife,
how to pucker and smile, how to make the most of eyelashes.

Last holiday her dear mother didn't recognize her
in among the city folk getting off the train.
You can tell by her shoes she's no country girl.

"And can you imagine walking home
in the muddy fields with these heels?"
she sings, as her number is called on the megaphone.

Lady recruitment officer asks if her book is a good one.
Su Ji nods firmly, "You know what it's like
working a plastic injection machine.

It never spits out the form until you've
twiddled the right buttons."
Su Ji's learning is paying off.

She's been hired again:
Assistant Sales Manager
for Silk Dragon Mobile Phones.

Years later, I run into Su Ji
on an all-expense cruise trip to Iceland.
We're here to see the aurora borealis,

the flickering of the sun's mood swings
playing with Earth's emotions
high upon the stratosphere.

She's wearing a sticker which reads:
Happy to meet you, I'm: MRS. DOLLY WU.
And she's decked out in ermine and mink.

Su Ji has a new nose and her hair is cut short
but I know it's her. Leaning against the railing
I ask if she's married a millionaire,

but she turns to face the cold ocean
as someone shouts: Killer whale!
and pretends not to know.

Mao Zedong Prefers Blondes

Just please don't squeeze the Chairman.
—Kissinger to Nixon

Men hover everywhere,
bullets aimed at the back of your mind;
as he reclines in resplendence deep in his velvet armchair
puffing on his Panda cigarettes.

He's small, you know;
not the towering monument you'd expect
from his blood-red posters and the sunshine behind his head
and he hides in the contours

of his suit like a big bad wolf
trapped in Grandma's body from a nursery rhyme,
shuffles in soft-padded shoes like slippers
and socks sheer as stockings reveal warts on his ankles,

but when he pierces you
with his glance, you know this is the man
a whole nation conjured in a dream. *Freedom is more
than the will of a people,* he says. *Freedom is measured in time.*

He's nasal; mousy, almost,
but that doesn't stop him from unwinding
all your preconceptions, running his little fingers through your hair;
before you know it, he's made you his plaything

and when you finally stand
before him, you won't think of a thing
to catch him off guard, reveal his dark secrets, like Nixon;
all you want to do is reach down and hug him like a teddy bear.

Monkeys & Flowers

Nobody stands for old Auntie
on the 6:45 to Purple Pagoda Park.

Most of us are gripping the overhead rails
like whooping monkeys.

In the streets of a city,
flowers need a man's attention.

There are no birds, no bees.
Dirt & dung are horse-carted

& the Buddha & the Chairman skip hand
in hand all the way down to the waterfront.

The Inevitability of Rice

Jack Wu, self-made multi-billion dollar rice tycoon says:

No, you can't go wrong with it.
Rice dries well and swells to three times its size.
It's the most flexible food the world ever had.
Provides nearly one quarter of the world's caloric intake.

And get this: it's a weed—cattle fodder.
So it grows almost anywhere.

Above his desk a placard reads:

GRAIN OF PORTENT

SMALLEST DIVISIBLE OBJECT

KERNEL OF PROFIT AND LOSS

INSPIRATION FOR THE FIRST COUP

EARLIEST CULTIVATED CROP

FEEDS BILLIONS

Jack smiles, claps me on the back:

Join hands with me on this.

We're growing so fast,
we'll soon be taking over the Earth!

Wall

This is the wall that contains history, he says,
kicking the brick with his boot.

*Without her we would have become
a kingdom of small-thinking.*

*She has made us, contained us, distilled us
into a hard liquid, the protectors of seas and rivers;*

*has given us our edge over the encroaching barbarians
who incessantly beat at the gate.*

This is the wall that holds in innocence, he says,
the purest nature of ourselves.

*She is the only man-made structure
you can see from the moon.*

Isn't she a wonder?

Demarcation Line

Imaginary. Lick of paint.
Chain-link fence.
No canonical Maginot Line.
Besides, you need to see

demons to subdue them.
Far better, the wall of the mind.
Walls crumble, but lines, lines can be
repainted again and again at little cost.

And remain broken. I've tried to cross
a hundred times. Sneaking behind
the guard post. Crawling through
barbed bracken. Burrowing beneath mole-like.

And once or twice I've nearly made it.
Just watch me walk down that narrow strip
of no man's land. Cross the line. Until, I'm just another
speck on the horizon.

Corruption

He steps out of the courthouse,
the guards his shadow dancers

locked in stride. We're throwing words at him,
words like stones, stones like words.

A Burberry raincoat
taut over his infamous head,

elbows like clipped wings,
someone in the crowd says

they discovered millions stashed
in his cousin's water silo in the countryside

where pigeons roost and shit.
Die, pig! shout the grandmas.

Good riddance! shout their husbands
stooped on walking sticks,

sitting on collapsible chairs,
as once they bellowed forty years before

when they were Red Guards
smashing priceless vases,

burning bourgeois novels,
chopping French furniture for firewood,

hanging Professor Liu
from his favorite willow tree

in the courtyard like wet laundry,
pounded on stones, like words

on the Emerald Lake
where a house burns,

where red-crowned cranes nest,
where they're washing their hands.

Yunnan Dragonfly

—for H.C.

How I should like to collide with a blue dragonfly

      while pedaling home in the soft shade of white pines

in the spring. And how too, I should like

      to witness its terrified eyes gleaming like little suns,

that I should know the world in the glance of an insect

      passing on into the eternity of Kunming dust.

Two tigers
Two tigers
Running fast
Running fast
One has no ears
One has no tail
Truly strange
Truly strange

Children's song, China

(Sung to the tune of *"Frère Jacques"*)

Fire Horse

Paint Hong Kong red from the earth to the sky.
—*Slogan plastered on the China Friendship Store, Hong Kong, 1967*

Hong Kong, 1966–1969

The years of the Cultural Revolution & over the border
children are soldiers.

A Fire Horse like your son, or so the Venerable Chan intones,
would burn a thousand bridges like Stalin

or raise them high over galactic distances like JFK. In those years
when over the border

children are soldiers, fathers & mothers are paraded and paddled
as examples of proletariat degeneracy

& we move to Stanley, beyond the Happy Valley, on the edge
of a fisherman's market

where they sell sea snakes by the dozen & clams the size of dinner
plates. It's here my old man smokes cigars

& learns strategies in the art of war & Mother learns to bake apple pie
with flaky Danish pastry from my nursemaid,

Amma Lui, who's worked in the kitchens of the Jockey Club.
While they plot & bake, the AC vent spits

hot air into our tropical garden. Outside among the rhododendrons
I ride my stick horse, Lightning,

running spears through hearts of cacti, eagerly watching
the thick white blood run all over the earth.

3:AM Interview: The Big Forgetting

Tom Bradley: China's long, nearly static history, climaxed with the past hundred years of political and economic upheavals, make for what must be the world's most difficult subject to treat exhaustively. But that is just what you have done in *Mao's Mole*. Did you set out to deal with the subject of national, racial and tribal metamorphosis, using China as an especially vivid and extreme example?

Marc Vincenz: Not at first. Individual pieces arrived sporadically: on the edges of dreams, were clipped from conversations in karaoke bars, on noodle stands, at the train station, arose as flashbacks of memories and past lives. Although each voice or image is singular, they are also born out of a communal mythology, a common "becoming"—in a way, the various characters stitched themselves together (some zigzagged, others loosely tacked themselves on). I was taken aback myself when I observed from a distance and watched the bigger picture come into focus.

About halfway through, I realized that *Mao's Mole* was about far more than just the individual narratives. Yes, there were individual stories, individual characters, but there was also a "basso ostinato" running through the heart of the book. Each of these individuals shared an embedded and deeply rooted commonality. It took me a while to figure out what exactly that was.

TB: Do you want to get explicit? Will you identify that commonality for us, or are we on our own?

MV: I am little skeptical of delving into the theory of my own creative work, but, ok, let me give it a go.

As rituals, icons, philosophies and myths move into a technological, economically-driven future, intentions are diffused; they are amended to fulfill revised- and cross-purposes; they become muddied or watered-down, reinterpreted or revised and evolve (or are evolved) to fit contemporary desires. In this manner, as civilizations evolve, so too do their mythologies—as their emperors, kings, priests, dictators and elected leaders reinvent religion and social structures. This mutated iconography (although seemingly from a distant past) embeds itself in a nation's revised (self-) consciousness, promising a better, more-balanced future with a faint whiff of the past. Perhaps this is the great deceit of what we call "civilization." In a layered papier-mâché of propaganda, rhetoric and perceived history, these symbols integrate into a single entity capable of feeding upon itself; just like the multiple-celled organism, civilization splits, conjoins, mutates and evolves with multiple adaptations on multiple islands.

Perhaps at its most basic level, *Mao's Mole* is a cinematic journey through China's last hundred-or-so years, offering snapshots, incidental reflections and moments of flux across a broad spectrum of the Middle Kingdom's citizens and their foreign guests. On wider levels, the book poses deep questions of society, identity and culture; *Mao's Mole* concerns itself with the development of icons, figureheads and modern mythology in today's China; with the making of modern nations; with our dented twenty-first century mythologies.

TB: It's an understatement to call *Mao's Mole* ambitious; yet the book holds together miraculously well. Each of the individual poems moves to the next according to an organizing principle that is so organic as to be suspected rather than discerned. Clearly, historical epochs, dynasties, and Five-Year Plans are part of the structure, but you have dispensed with mere chronology, to offer a deeper series of connections. Can you reveal something of your framework here, to the extent it was consciously built?

MV: Although mostly portrayed as such, history, of course is actually non-linear—at the very least in the way we perceive it. Surely personal memory and "real" history are intertwined, become distorted or magnified. I mean how much do any of us remember of our earliest years of childhood? Perhaps we recall a handful of significant moments, but are these recollections really the way things happened?

Yes, it was very tempting to follow that straight arrow of time, but it's really the crucial moments, the so-called epiphanies, the turning points that create change and paint a personal history in the mind's inner eye.

On another level, I realized that each of these narratives represented some of those moments that were missing from documented history—moments that would likely never receive public attention, rather part of what someone once termed, "the big forgetting." How could these multiple journeys of so many individuals be portrayed in a linear fashion? It seemed implausible; after all, it was these individual "little epiphanies" (or little deaths) that stitched the book together, that created what you have called the organic (or perhaps biometric) structure.

And yes, just as the Chinese Communist Party's Five-Year Plan, is a work in five movements; each movement represents an era or a wave of social, economic or emotional transition that, in turn, is followed by singular passages of discord, dispersion, acceptance and assimilation. Underpinned by the faux poetry of Mao's propaganda, each of these movements is expressed in a layering of reflections, narratives, slogans, images, quips and asides, as a multitude of individual voices merge into one tentative organism.

Another way of thinking of the structure is to envision as a Philip Stark score in five movements—with brief intermezzos between each major movement. Like Stark, these movements begin with a simple melodic phrase, but slowly, as more tones underlay the melody, it expands, divests, until, despite (or in spite of) the ambient noise (the background radiation), the original phrase reverberates somewhere in the subconscious.

TB: Mao himself is the Moses of this Pentateuch, the Christ of this Gospel. You don't respect him overmuch as a poet, but you have spelunked his labyrinthine character and provided a psychological portrait that rivals any yet written in prose, fiction or non-. Can you talk about your conception of him as man and myth?

MV: Even the most evil genius, is a genius. Aside from Confucius and Lao Tze, Mao is without a shadow of a doubt, China's most famous son. He's been compared to Hitler, Stalin, Bonaparte, Tamerlane, Ghengis Khan, yet he portrayed himself as a reactionary poet, a sensitive scholar and, at the same time, he portrayed himself as a man of the common folk. We know enough now from the multitude of biographies and a few dissident former Party members who have come out of the closet (and haven't been "taken out") that he was nothing like a common man. He lived the lush life of an emperor.

And even after all of his disasters and catastrophes, he's still hailed as a demigod; the ultimate symbol of Chinese independence and nationalism.

Not so long ago, I asked a Beijing friend of mine if she thought his portrait might one day be taken down from Tiananmen Square. She smiled wryly and told me that it would be utterly unthinkable. Imagine if Hitler's portrait still stared down at you from the Brandenburg Gate—that too is unthinkable. It would defy all moral sensibilities and common sense; yet Mao, the demigod, watches over his people, above the gates of the fallen "Emperor's" Forbidden City. If you wouldn't know better you'd think there was some kind of a sick inside joke going on.

TB: And Mao fuels the book's momentum?

MV: Loosely speaking. Each of *Mao's Mole's* movements is derived from Mao's own propaganda machine—as his empire rises and falls, and rises and falls again. The book closes with the foreshadowing of a probable Second Coming—and just as other civilizations have begged their gods return, so too Mao's spirit is requested to arise and lead his good comrades back into the red light, into the good fight.

TB: One of the great delights of this collection is the cast of characters, each drawn with the detail and depth one usually associates with novels. Of course, each story is unique and worthy of being told in its own right, but tell us who some of your favorite characters are, and what function you see them serving in the greater structure.

MV: I suppose it's only through this wily and varied cast of characters that the true picture can emerge. No, no favorite. They all have their role to play.

TB: How about if I suggest some of my own favorites? I am thinking of the young man in "The Analects of Wu Wei: Virtuous Dog Meat," who extolls the Taoist virtues of eating dog while driving to work in a Mercedes. Another vivid personage is the eponymous "Citizen Julius Wong," the one-armed ex-Communist Party cadre now settled on the island of Fiji, who advises rebel generals and swims with parrot fish. There's the "Tai Chi Master" who practices his art to produce nuclear fission; Lu Xi, the poor factory line worker in "Legs, Hands, Fingers," who has lost the feeling in her hands and believes herself to be transforming into a serpent: and the businessman in "While Facing the Urinal" who is offered an assassin's services while trying to urinate.

MV: Yes, these are all people struggling to come to terms with the same morphing mythology: five-thousand-plus years of history condensed in the metaphor of the Cultural Revolution—a quintessential "rethinking" of all that ever was.

Each character, phrase or passage is a symbolically linked thread of a continually evolving web of convention, misinformation and misconstruction—and yet, each of these individual's fates are reflected in some skewed sense of the primordial in a modern beauty: one among many nations facing a schizophrenic future.

TB: You know China at all levels, as only an expatriate can, and an adventurous expatriate at that. If you think it won't taint readers' enjoyment of , please tell us voyeurs something about any autobiographical truck you might have had with the Flowery Middle Kingdom: formative prepubescent traumas, travels, misadventures, Sino-fornication and so forth. For example, I have heard that you were actually born in the neighborhood, and at a key moment in their history.

MV: I don't know about all levels. I don't believe anyone can ever no a place, a race, a tribe or a nation, and particularly one as vast, varied and ancient as China. Expatriate? Maybe. But then again, I was born in the Middle Kingdom, so does that make me Chinese?—if not in race or culture, perhaps in spirit? You'd have to ask my Chinese friends.

Shortly after I came into the world, Mao's Cultural Revolution was
in full-on class struggle behind the bamboo curtain. Even in our
"colonial jewel" that was Hong Kong, Maoist separatists were chanting
revolutionary slogans outside capitalist factories, planting bombs down
at Victoria Harbor, tossing Molotov cocktails into bourgeois shop fronts.

Mum's father (I called him Gung Gung, the Cantonese for grandfather)
had been posted to the colony just after World War II. His official task
was to map Hong Kong and all its outlying islands and territories; as I
came to find out later, his unofficial detail was to keep an eye out for
revolutionary activities in border areas. Gung Gung was one of the very
few British government employees given permission to learn what the
other civil servants called "a rather distasteful tongue."

TB: Some of the most fascinating poems in the book pertain to
the pursuit of capitalist enterprises deep inside the world's hugest
communist dictatorship. What is your background in this delicate field
of endeavor?

MV: My own father entered into a business partnership with a Shanghai
businessman who had a penchant for bloody steaks and Peking Opera,
and, who had fled China's Revolution in the 50s. Strangely, despite his
having fled the Republic, this Shanghai businessman still had notable
connections within the Party. He and Dad built a business selling
raw materials (from as far afield as the US, Canada, Brazil, Chile,
South Africa and Tasmania) to the Communist Party and its singular
ministries. (In those days all business in China was centralized: one
ministry, one commodity.)

No matter where we lived—Hong Kong, Zurich, New York, London—
there was hardly a month we didn't have a cadre or comrade visiting
our home (My mother made sure we had a good stock of corn on
the cob. It seemed to be a Party favorite.) Already in these years, the
late 60s and 70s, Mao's Party Line crept surreptitiously into our daily
conversations. And in the 80s, when we lived in Connecticut and Dad

was working in New York, we were sure our phone lines were being tapped on both sides. At his offices, Dad regularly received regular visits from Men in Black. An on-going family joke was a question that had been frequently posed to Dad: "Mr. Vincenz are you a member of the Communist Party?"

In the 90s, after having worked for businesses in Hong Kong and China myself, I finally ventured it on my own. I spent the good part of the late 90s and early 2000s living and working in and out of Shanghai and Beijing where I reluctantly tumbled headfirst into the growing economic powerhouse that China was starting to become. Despite the echoes of Tiananmen, Deng Xiao Ping's "Get Rick Quick" scheme had taken firm hold. Possibly one of the first lessons I learned first-hand is that in China absolutely nothing is ever as it seems.

TB: Your poetry derives richness and energy from the gigantic contradictions China poses on the world stage. How do you manage to draw such immediate and personal poetry from these vast economic, political and historical tectonics?

MV: China is, of course, one of the most culturally and historically significant civilizations on our planet, and has much to offer the open-minded, yet even now, the shadow of Mao's legacy hangs heavy over the Middle Kingdom. Guy Sorman, French economist and sinologist has said: "The Propaganda Department functions with ruthless efficiency, making gullible foreigners accept unquestioningly whatever it chooses to put out: economic statistics that cannot be verified, trumped-up elections, blanked-out epidemics, imaginary labor harmony, and the purported absence of any aspiration for democracy."

Of course, you can never know a people or a nation. And despite my many experiences within China and with her citizens, I will always remain an outsider; yet my impressions of these people, their landscapes, heartaches and laughter—and, above all, their on-going attempt to come to grips with an ancient legacy, with Communist doubletalk and the current Party's proto-Marxist capitalism (a dichotomy if ever there was one)—continues to baffle and astound me.

I lived close to my Chinese colleagues and friends, broke bread with them, shared tears with them, consoled and laughed with them. How could I not become personally entangled in their lives? Although few of the poems refer to specific people (you know who you are), all of them are shadows or ghosts of people I have known on some level.

TB: So the Cultural Revolution is a metaphor, then?

MV: Absolutely. I have come to see this ultra-rapid, development of the Chinese nation from a country of emperors and robber barons, through Mao's Cultural Revolution, to its present "economic coming of age" as a metaphor for the development of modern "civilization". In many ways what China has survived in the last forty years is much akin to Europe's Industrial Revolution of the mid-Nineteenth Century. And despite the fact that much of the western world believes China is on a narrow path to taking over the global economy, one must bear in mind that 80% of China's population still lives in abject poverty. The money and power remains in the hands of the few—most of them well intertwined in the CCP, the Chinese Communist Party—China's modern emperors and warlords.

TB: One is put in mind of your Revolutionary Commander, merciful and jocular, who addresses his troops in the penultimate poem of section one.

MV: Right. In China today, you experience the greatest extremes of wealth and poverty, injustice and indifference. For me, *Mao's Mole* is not just about China's recent history, but about how time and again, myth is being reinvented to serve the purposes of the powers-that-be under the guise of modernizing a nation.

Acknowledgements

I would like to thank the editors of the following publications in which these poems, sometimes in different versions, appeared.

Spillway Review: "Quest"
Pirene's Fountain: "Crushed Dragon Bones"
Ferlingue: "Barbers"
Stirring: "Suzie Lam Scorns the Happy Marriage Dating Agency"
    and "Bicycle"
nthposition: "No Birds"
Nibble: "She Thinks I Look Like Lenin"
Frostwriting: "The Price of Humidity"
Cha: An Asian Literary Journal: "Hunchback Rat of the Red Star Hotel"
Sein und Werden: "Building a Japanese Butterfly"
Inertia: "Citizen Julius Wong"
Rumble: "Legs, Hands, Fingers"
The Literary Bohemian: "Word of Advice from Blue Moon Rising"
APT: "Scaling the Great Wall of Joy"
Poets & Artists: "Base Pairs"
The Nervous Breakdown: "Mole"
Ducts Journal and *Poets for Living Waters:* "The River, Once"
MiPOesias: "The General's Little Panda Paws"
Right Hand Pointing: "Tai C'hi Master"
Lantern Review: "Taishan Mountain"
OKNO: "Taishan Mountain" translated into the Russian by Jenya Krein
Steaua Journal and Agentia de Carte: "Taishan Mountain," "No
Birds" and "Xiao Hong's Great Leap Forward" translated into the
Romanian by Marius Surleac
Poetry Scotland (Open Mouse): "Girl on the Corner of Chang'An Street"
The Potomac: "Corruption"
Right Hand Pointing: "Wall"
Fleeting: "While Facing the Urinal"
Truck: "Monkeys & Flowers"
Connotation Press: "Abominable Kingdom"
Currency: "Stacks and Smokes"
Revolution House: "Fire Horse" and "K.Y."

Unlikely Stories: "The Red Underpants"
The Green Door: "Wushu" and "Unseen"
The St. Petersburg Review: "Kowtow"
Mobius: The Journal of Social Change: "Advanced Tree-Planting"
FRIGG: "The Mystical Art of Accounting"
    and "Swinging Swords in the Park"
Altered Scale: "The Smell of an Elevator" and "The Interrogatory"

The following poems appeared in the chapbook *Upholding Half the Sky*, published as part of the MiPOesias chapbook series by GOSS185: Casa Menendez (USA, 2010): "Building a Japanese Butterfly," "No Birds," "She Thinks I Look Like Lenin," "Base Pairs," "The General's Little Panda Paws," "Citizen Julius Wang," "Ling Guo Whispers (Building C4 Apartment F12-03)," "Thick End of a Camel's Tail," "Seepage" and "Moonlight Bebop."

The following poems appeared in the chapbook *The Propaganda Factory, or Speaking of Trees*, originally released by Argotist Ebooks as an e-book (UK, 2011), re-released in print by Spuyten Duyvil (New York, 2013): "Taishan Mountain," "Suzie Lam Scorns the Happy Marriage Dating Agency," "Manchurian Fog," "No Birds," "Base Pairs," "Thick End of a Camel's Tail," "Wall," "Monkey Brains," "Seepage," and "The River, Once."

"Tai C'hi Master," "Indefinite Measures," and "Stacks and Smokes" appeared in the chapbook *Pull of the Gravitons* (Right Hand Pointing, 2012).

"Deft" appears in *Gods of a Ransacked Century* (Unlikely Books, 2013);

Several of these poems were broadcasted by Tom Lodge on Radio Caroline.

"The River, Once" appears in *Poets for Living Waters: An Anthology* (Blazevox, 2013).

"Crushed Dragon Bones" appears in the anthology *Rhino in A Disappearing World* (Poet's Printery, S.Africa, 2013).

"The Big Forgetting" interview by Tom Bradley (3AM Magazine, 2013)

"Another Satisfied Customer" (MatterMonthly.com, 2013)

For support, encouragement and advice I would like to thank: Martin Espada, Jeramy Dodds, Inga Maria Brynjarsdottir, Leon Dewan, Carolyn Zukowski, F.J. Bergmann, Robin Vaughn-Williams, Jake Berry, Stacey Tsourounis, Tony Ontita, Tammy Ho-Lai Ming, Markus Bundi, Ernst Halter, Tom Bradley, Carol Novack, Josip Novakovich, Robin Robertson, Cornelius Eady, Ed Pavlic, Larissa Shmailo, Eric Tucker, Susan Scutti, Tod Thilleman, Mikhail Iossel, Susan Lewis, Jonathan Penton, Jeff Davis, Javier Blanco, Tim and Andrea Hamilton-Fletcher, Philip Nikolayev, Katia Kapovich, Allison Hedge Coke, Andreas Neeser, Ben Mazer, Didi Menendez, Ann Bogle, S.S. Liu, Raphael Moser, Andrei Codrescu, Wang Ping, Terese Svoboda, Marius Surleac, Gene Tanta, Jeffrey Side, Marcus Speh, Judith Kerman, the man who wore the paper bag, Joe Green, the Lone Ranger, Mr. "Put You in Da Caassbookt" Kwok, Ah Fuk, Pedro and Carmen Monjo, Fortunato, Stone, Tom Lodge, Guðbjörg Sveinsdóttir, the GSIS, Charles Tyler, Reynolds Price, James Applewhite, Adrian Marquez, Tedd Determann, Yuseff El Guindi, Alberto at the Casino Bar, and Zepp at the City Café.

Much heartfelt gratitude to Dale Winslow, Stephen Roxborough and Milo Duffin.

About the Author

Born in Hong Kong during the height of the Cultural Revolution, Marc Vincenz has spent most of his life on the road. He has lived in England, Switzerland, Spain, Hong Kong, China, the United States, and has traveled far and wide to such remote locations such as central Siberia, the Amazon Rainforest, Tibet, India's Thar Desert, and China's Kun Lun Mountains. After many years of business and travel in the Far East, he finally settled in Shanghai in the 90s.

Many years before this, he graduated from Duke University with a BA in Creative Writing, studied under notable authors such as Reynolds Price and Ariel Dorfman, and received the *Sudler Award for Outstanding Creative Achievement.*

His work has appeared in many journals both online and in print, including *Washington Square Review, Fourteen Hills, The Canary, The Bitter Oleander, Crab Creek Review, Tears in the Fence, Pirene's Fountain, Exquisite Corpse, The Potomac, Poetry Salzburg Review, Spillway, Stirring, MiPOesias* and *Guernica.* He has been nominated many times for the Pushcart prize and several times for Best of the Net. He has been awarded several grants from the Swiss Arts Council for his translations.

His recent books include *The Propaganda Factory, or Speaking of Trees; Pull of the Gravitons* and *Gods of a Ransacked Century* (Unlikely Books, 2013). A new English-German bi-lingual collection, *Additional Breathing Exercises,* is forthcoming from Wolfbach Verlag, Zurich, Switzerland (2014). His most recent translations include *Kissing Nests* by Werner Lutz and *Nightshift / An Area of Shadows* by Erika Burkart and Ernst Halter (both Spuyten Duyvil, 2013) and *Secret Letter* by Erika Burkart, (Cervena Barva Press, 2013).

He is currently working on a book-length alchemical poem tentatively entitled, *The Chymical Illuminations;* translating the works of Herman Hesse prizewinner, Klaus Merz; and completing a spoken-word album to be released by Neuroshell Records, New York.

Marc works as a poet, writer, journalist, editor, book designer, and creative consultant, and now divides his time between Reykjavik, Zurich, Berlin and New York City. He is Executive Editor of *MadHat (Mad Hatters' Review)* and MadHat Press and Coeditor-in-Chief of *Fulcrum.*

NeoPoiesis: *a new way of making*

1) in ancient Greece, poiesis referred to the
process of making: creation - production -
organization - formation - causation

2) a process that can be physical and
spiritual, biological and intellectual,
artistic and technological, material and
teleological, efficient and formal

3) a means of modifying the environment
and a method of organizing the self,
the making of art and music and poetry,
the fashioning of memory and history and
philosophy, the construction of perception
and expression and reality

4) an independent publisher with a steadfast
goal to print and promote outstanding
poets, writers and artists that reflect
the creative drive and spirit of the new
electronic landscape

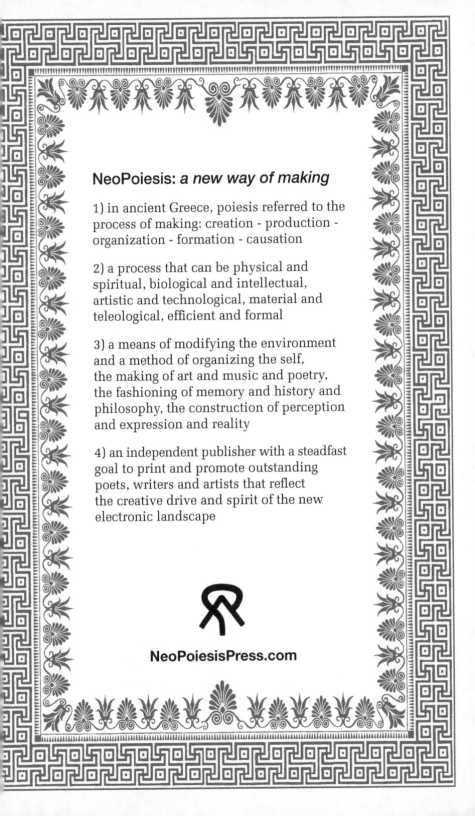

NeoPoiesisPress.com